TWAYNE'S WORLD AUTHORS SERIES

A Survey of the World's Literature

Sylvia E. Bowman, Indiana University
GENERAL EDITOR

SPAIN

Gerald Wade, Vanderbilt University
EDITOR

Federico García Lorca

TWAS 23

*TW*AYNE'S WORLD AUTHORS SERIES (TWAS)

*The purpose of TWAS is to survey the major writers
—novelists, dramatists, historians, poets, philosophers,
and critics—of the nations of the world. Among the
national literatures covered are those of Australia,
Canada, China, Eastern Europe, France, Germany,
Greece, India, Italy, Japan, Latin America, New Zea-
land, Poland, Russia, Scandinavia, Spain, and the
African nations, as well as Hebrew, Yiddish, and
Latin Classical literatures. This survey is comple-
mented by Twayne's United States Authors Series
and English Authors Series.*

*The intent of each volume in these series is to present
a critical-analytical study of the works of the writer;
to include biographical and historical material that
may be necessary for understanding, appreciation,
and critical appraisal of the writer; and to present all
material in clear, concise English—but not to vitiate
the scholarly content of the work by doing so.*

Federico García Lorca

By CARL W. COBB

University of Tennessee

TWAYNE PUBLISHERS
A DIVISION OF G. K. HALL & CO., BOSTON

MANUFACTURED IN THE UNITED STATES OF AMERICA

For my son Kim, whose presence has been my richest blessing, and for the mother who gave him birth.

Contents

Preface

IT WAS on the morning of August 19, 1936, that Federico García Lorca died before a firing squad near his home in Granada; and, since he perished under such circumstances, the critics have had difficulty in reaching an objective critical appraisal of his work. Lorca* had achieved an international reputation as a popular poet after the publication of his *Gypsy Ballads* (*Romancero gitano*) in 1928, a reputation which persisted in spite of his later change of poetic direction and of his protestations that he was not a poet of the people. After he was killed in early maturity at the beginning of the Spanish Civil War, Lorca quickly became a symbol of the best of Spanish tradition. His contemporaries, especially his fellow artists and critics, most of them confessing that they were overwhelmed by the force of his personality, have created a monument of biographical and critical materials which present adequately the Lorca of Spanish tradition. With the passing of time, however, it has become obvious that García Lorca's work as a whole has dimensions which tend to make him a modern European poet and dramatist as well, that is, in certain ways in rebellion against his own culture.

We believe that the reader who approaches his work without presuppositions will ultimately come to the conclusion that there is a basic duality in García Lorca, both in his life and his work. After gaining his reputation with the *Gypsy Ballads*, which many thought were poems of the local color of Andalusia, Lorca initiated an almost complete change of direction in *Poet in New York* (*Poeta en Nueva York*), a book of radical form and vanguard theme, which disconcerted many critics. The Spanish critics, of

* According to Spanish custom, the poet's name would be properly García Lorca. However, the poet frequently refers to himself as Lorca, as do many critics.

course, early became aware of the duality and conflicts in Lorca, but have preferred to stress the traditional and to draw away from the iconoclastic elements, so that a note of evasiveness has crept into much of their criticism. And the more conservative of the critics, while stressing Lorca as a popular poet, have managed subtly to attack even his poetry supposedly written in the popular manner. Perhaps surprisingly, literary historian Angel Valbuena Prat has questioned the permanence of the poetic method in the *Gypsy Ballads,* probably Lorca's most enduring book. Another eminent critic, Guillermo Díaz-Plaja, has also appraised this book in a lukewarm manner. The Spanish critics in general, with an eye on Lorca's international reputation, have tried sincerely to enhance the poet's position without clarifying the psychological bases for the tensions and conflicts which give his work power. In the final analysis, what this reluctance to endorse Lorca's work means is that the Spanish critics have been unable to accept his serious iconoclastic aspects, those which have clashed with Spanish tradition.

In 1956 the problems in interpreting Lorca were brought to a head when Jean-Louis Schonberg, a French professor, in a biographical and critical study of Lorca's work, accused the Spanish critics of glossing over extremely important details of Lorca's life and consequently of obscuring the poet's purpose in his work. Why, asked Schonberg, had there been a "conspiracy of silence" among Lorca's contemporaries concerning details of his life? Why had there been such reluctance in printing some of his manuscripts? Schonberg attempted to prove why by presenting a biography written frankly but without sensationalism. Although his book has been met with stony silence or cries of rage, we feel that Schonberg's reading of many of Lorca's poems, even some of the well-known ballads, is at least a logical starting point. Admittedly Schonberg sometimes fails to relate Lorca's homosexual attitudes properly to his work, but his book, which no one has tried to refute, is a major contribution to a more complete evaluation of Lorca's work.

As Schonberg emphasized, García Lorca's relations with the painter Salvador Dalí are of great importance in his life and work. Although six years younger than Lorca, Dalí, from his youth a rebel, consistently scandalized conservative Spain and was ultimately rejected almost totally, so that he went to France and did much of his mature work there. During the years 1921–28, Lorca and Dalí were very close, both personally and as artists. Their central impulse was toward freedom, freedom to throw off all the shackles binding total expression of the personality, including even scatological and sexual taboos. Dalí came to represent for Lorca the influence of the Catalonian group which from Barcelona attempted to import and develop Freudian and surrealist ideas from France and the rest of Europe. García Lorca was therefore a poet between two worlds, the traditional Spanish and the modern Eurpean, and we propose to study him by stressing his real achievements in both worlds.

In a general study of this type, we acknowledge our indebtedness to the critical and biographical materials which have appeared over the years. The studies of Del Río, Díaz-Plaja, Arturo Berenguer-Carísomo, Roberto Sánchez and the others listed in our bibliography have much merit; what we may consider their shortcomings are due, not to incompetence, but to Spanish reticence. We have attempted to utilize the primary and secondary biographical sources available. In addition to Schonberg's book, the critical biography of Fernando Vázquez Ocaña, in which he collected and ordered almost all the biographical materials available, has been very helpful. We have tried to give proper credit and suggestions for further reading in the Notes, but lack of space reduces our opportunity to acknowledge the work of other Lorquian scholars.

We have departed slightly from what has become the usual formula in discussing Lorca's work. Since we believe that his *Gypsy Ballads* and *Poet in New York* are the books crucial to his enduring reputation, we have devoted chapters to them, with an attempt to analyze as many individual poems as possible. We have endeavored to respect Lorca's intentions, but we realize that his poetry is complex enough to provide more than one kind of interpretation. Refusing to hide behind generalities as some critics have done, we have perhaps erred in some instances. The reader who first tries to encompass a book like *Poet in New York* will realize Lorca's complexity, but he should remember that Lorca wrote nothing deliberately incoherent.

The ultimate aim of a book of the present type is of course to encourage the reader to take up the *Complete Works* of Lorca and attempt to reach a full understanding of his original talents. As a master of metaphor and imagery, Lorca is almost unrivaled in his ability to transmute the materials of tradition and of his own experience into a poetic expression of his personality. Since the traditions which he utilizes are typically Spanish, he must be read in the original for full appreciation, as indeed any fine poet should be. Although Ben Belitt's translation of *Poet in New York* is adequate, Lorca's poetry in traditional form has been translated wretchedly, in spite of the fact that we have a tradition in English from which to work, especially the ballads of A. E. Housman. Usually we have preferred our own versions of fragments quoted in this book, with an awareness that most of them can be improved.

García Lorca is a difficult but a rewarding poet. As the continued growth of his international reputation perhaps indicates, he is strongly representative of the sensibility of our times. Although there is little joy or tranquillity or affirmation in his poetry and drama, Lorca, with his prophetically tragic outlook, infused into his work the turbulence, rebellion and frustration of spirit of the modern age. At the time of his death he was struggling to return to his people and Spanish tradition, to become the universal voice of the Spanish spirit. That spirit was subjected to probably its sternest test in the chaos of the Civil War which claimed him as a victim. Because of his tragic death, García Lorca remains a symbol of the dreadful tension between creation and destruction which continues to beset our world today.

CARL W. COBB

University of Tennessee

Acknowledgments

Federico García Lorca, SELECTED POEMS. Copyright 1955 by New Directions Publishing Corporation. Reprinted by permission of New Directions Publishing Corporation, New York.

I gratefully acknowledge the permission of the poet's sister, Isabel García Lorca, to quote from the *Obras completas,* especially the poems, "Arbolé, arbolé" and the "Romance sonámbulo."

I am indebted to the Cooperative Program in the Humanities at the University of North Carolina in Chapel Hill and to Furman University for making possible my year's work in the libraries at Chapel Hill and at Duke University in Durham.

Finally, I am deeply grateful to Dr. Gerald E. Wade for his help with the manuscript.

Chronology

1898   Federico García Lorca born June 5 in Fuentevaqueros, near Granada.

1898–   Years of childhood in Fuentevaqueros and Valderrubio.
1908

1909   Family moves to Granada.

1914   Lorca begins study of Law in University of Granada.

1918   Publishes his first book, *Impressions and Landscapes* (*Impresiones y paisajes*). First dated poems.

1919–   Begins his stay at the Residence of Students in Madrid.
1928

1920   Stages his first drama, *The Evil-doing of the Butterfly* (*El Maleficio de la mariposa*).

1921   Publishes first *Book of Poems* (*Libro de poemas*), written 1917–1921. Begins *Poem of the Deep Song* (*Poema del cante jondo*), to be published in 1931.

1924   Begins the *Gypsy Ballads* (*Romancero gitano*), published in 1928. Working on *Songs* (*Canciones*), to be published in 1927; *Mariana Pineda*, to be premiered in 1927 in Barcelona and in Madrid.

1925   First visit to Cadaqués with Salvador Dalí.

1926   Writes essay "The Poetic Image in Don Luis de Góngora" (*La imagen poética en don Luis de Góngora*). Publishes "Ode to Salvador Dalí" (*Oda a Salvador Dalí*) in the *Revista de Occidente*. Writes first version of *The Shoemaker's Prodigious Wife* (*La Zapatera prodigiosa*), to be premiered in 1930, restaged in 1935.

1927   Exhibits his drawings in Barcelona in June. Journeys with other poets to Seville in celebration of Góngora.

1928   Edits the magazine *Cock* (*Gallo*). Publishes the *Gypsy Ballads* (*Romancero gitano*) in April. Writes *Love of Don*

Perlimplín (*Amor de Don Perlimplín*), later staged (in 1933) in Madrid. Writes *The Sketch of Don Christopher* (*El Retablillo de Don Cristóbal*), to be staged in 1935.

1929– Arrives in New York in June. Works on *Thus Five Years*
1930 *Pass* (*Así que pasen cinco años*) and *The Public* (*El Público*), the former to be privately staged in 1936. Writes first version of *Yerma*, later revised and premiered (in December, 1934) in Madrid. Writes the poems of *Poet in New York* (*Poeta en Nueva York*), individual poems to be published in 1931, public reading by Lorca, 1931, finally published in Spanish and English, 1940. Reads his essay "Theory and Function of the Daemon" (*Teoría y juego del duende*) in Cuba.

1931 Begins the *Divan of Tamarit* (*Diván del Tamarit*), to be published in 1936. Begins work with university theater group *La Barraca*.

1932 Writes *Blood Wedding* (*Bodas de sangre*), to be premiered in Madrid in 1933. Works with *La Barraca*.

1933 Journeys to Argentina for productions of *Blood Wedding*, *Mariana Pineda* and *The Shoemaker's Prodigious Wife*, reading of a group of essays. Publishes "Ode to Walt Whitman" (*Oda a Walt Whitman*) in Mexico.

1934 Writes the *Lament for the Death of a Bullfighter* (*Llanto por Ignacio Sánchez Mejías*), to be published in 1935.

1935 Writes *Doña Rosita the Spinster* (*Doña Rosita la Soltera*), premiered in Barcelona in December. Publishes *Six Poems in Galician* (*Seis poemas gallegos*).

1936 Publishes *First Songs* (*Primeras canciones*), which had been written in 1922. Writes *The House of Bernarda Alba* (*La casa de Bernarda Alba*), not to be staged until 1945 in Buenos Aires, in Madrid in 1950. Returns to Granada in July. Taken into custody and shot on the morning of August 19, 1936.

CHAPTER 1

Life and Times of Federico García Lorca

I The Historical and Cultural Background

THE year 1898, the date of the birth of Federico García Lorca, was a significant one for Spanish history and letters. In the brief months of the Spanish American War Spain lost Cuba and the Philippines, the remnants of an empire on which the sun never set. At the turn of the century, two general groups were competing in Spain: one sought to Europeanize Spain, to introduce scientific advances and cultural ideas; the other to turn inward and toward the past to discover the eternal Spanish tradition. While the motto of the novelist and dramatist Benito Pérez Galdós had been "Forward," the eminent man of letters Miguel de Unamuno (1864–1936) chose as his watchword "Inward." Unamuno and the group of authors beginning to mature at the turn of the last century have come to be called the Generation of 1898.

The majority of the members of this Generation, although not originally from Castile, chose generally to defend the ideals of this central and key province, and the spirit of the immortal Don Quixote became the inspiration for the group. The major figure, the Basque Unamuno, in a collection of essays, novels, poems and plays, struggled to save his Catholic faith against rationalistic philosophy, to assert the importance of the individual soul against the rise of mass movements and to restore Spain's eminence in Europe, not through political power but with the indomitable Spanish spirit. A major novelist of the group was Pío Baroja, another Basque, who, in a long series of novels, analyzed and generally assailed the (to him) outmoded Spanish culture and its institutions. Another of the Generation, the Galician Ramón del Valle-Inclán, passed in his evolution as a writer through a period of elegant decadence and finally created a manner called *esperpento*, grotesque deformation of reality cast in various literary genres. He also wrote a series of novelized dramas called *Barbaric*

Comedies, in which he traced the development of a great family. The foremost dramatist of the Group was Jacinto Benavente, Nobel Prize winner in 1922, who dominated the Spanish theater for years with plays of urbane social comment, but with an occasional departure like the rural tragedy *The Passion Flower* (*La malquerida*), a type of drama later exploited by Lorca.

The outstanding poets of the period were Antonio Machado and Juan Ramón Jiménez, another winner of the Nobel Prize for Literature. Jiménez, beginning as an impressionist and often writing in popular forms such as the ballad, became the champion of pure poetry early in the century. Antonio Machado, a profound and thoughtful poet, in addition to composing poems of popular themes and forms, wrote sensitive poetry on the Castilian landscape and ultimately began to reflect the new philosophical currents of Europe. All these and many others of the gifted Generation of 1898 continued to write throughout the period of Lorca's youth and early manhood.

The Generation of 1898 was important to Lorca's Generation of 1927 in certain basic ways. First, the members set high artistic and critical standards. Moreover, during the course of one generation this group, generally speaking, abandoned the Catholic orthodoxy which had prevailed in Spain. While Unamuno was vitally concerned with faith, even he was often criticized for the unorthodox expression of his beliefs. Jiménez deliberately avoided Christian doctrine, and Baroja was a bitter critic of Spanish Catholicism. Baroja and others were particularly critical of the schools run by the religious orders, especially the Jesuits, and their effect on the personalities of the youth in the schools. This group also persistently re-worked the Don Juan theme to criticise various aspects of the social structure in Spain. Unamuno, Machado and Azorín sought to rediscover the Spanish landscape, to focus on the individuality of specific provinces and to transmute their observations into first-rate literature. The ideal of a cultural rebirth in Spain as expressed by Unamuno naturally involved as a first step reasoned criticism of the existing situation in order to create a program to arrest Spain's decline.

II *Lorca's Youth in Granada*

Although he himself caused a confusion of long standing by giving an incorrect date, Federico García Lorca was born on June 5, 1898, at Fuentevaqueros near Granada, as publication of his birth certificate has confirmed. His father, Don Federico García Rodríguez, a well-to-do landowner, was an unaffected, kind, generous man, faithful to the paternalistic traditions of rural Andalusia. After his first wife died, in 1897 he had married doña Vicenta Lorca, then a teacher in the town. The fact that Lorca's mother doña Vicenta was his father's second wife was strangely important to Lorca, for he remembered later that his infancy was an "obsession with a silver service and some portraits of that one who could have been my mother." [1] It was doña Vicenta who taught Federico the alphabet and his first lessons in music. From her, he felt he had received his intelligence and his artistic inclinations; from his father, his passionate nature.

According to various testimonies, Lorca was a precocious and sensitive child who had a number of early problems. At two months he had suffered a grave illness. There is mention of his tendency toward quietness and withdrawal, of sometimes "seeing visions." His mother consistently took him to Mass, and the various elements of the service had a profound impression on him. During one period, his favorite game involved the improvisation of an altar at which he said Mass for the members of his family, especially his younger brother, Francisco, and his two younger sisters. He remained interested in the drama from the day a group came to the village and set up a puppet show. Federico, enchanted with the performance, eventually constructed his own set of marionettes and presented original performances for the neighbors. He later recalled that he was sent to a school in Almería, but suffered a grave throat illness and had to be brought home. Lorca remembered years later how his mother had strongly favored him on account of his delicate health.

Around 1909, Federico's family moved to Granada. Apparently at this time he wanted to be a musician and composer; his practical father, who wanted him to study law, sent him to the College of the Sacred Heart to prepare for the University. In the *colegio* Federico was exposed to the ancient system of teaching which

Vázquez Ocaña calls "scholastic pragmatism," a system based on Aquinas, which attempts to harmonize positive, or utilitarian, Catholic thought with a certain form of mysticism.[2] This system clashed with the rationalistic pragmatism as defended by the intellectuals Giner and Cossío, a pragmatism based in part on the newer ideas of progress through science and contemporary social ideas. All the writers of the Generation of 1898 felt this powerful clash of ideologies as young men, and the majority of them could never return to their traditional Catholic faith. Lorca felt the faith emotionally, but pursued freedom of action and thought to their logical limits. As had many generations before him, he endured the teaching, always interested in a thousand other things, and was graduated from the *colegio* in 1914.

Lorca was enrolled immediately in the University of Granada to study simultaneously in the schools of Law and Liberal Arts (*Filosofía y Letras*). He never became a serious student, and failed three courses in the University, one of them in literature. Already, however, he revealed an excessive desire to attract attenion, since he remembered later that he gained considerable popularity by coining clever nicknames for everyone. During these years he continued the serious study of music. While enrolled at the University Lorca developed a pattern of living not related directly to his studies. Around 1916, he and a group of friends began to frequent one of the cafés in Granada. Then and later Lorca spent much time in this environment; apparently with his wit and conversational magic he was usually the leader of his group. Generally much of the conversation involved the wide gulf between the group and the rest of the stodgy, pedantic, workaday world, whose members Lorca cleverly denominated *los putrefactos*, "the putrefied ones."

During this period Lorca came under the influence of two important men who played a part in his development. One was the eminent musician Manuel de Falla, whose reputation had been sealed recently with the presentation of *Love the Magician* (*El amor brujo*) in Madrid. De Falla was obviously impressed by the interest and talent of young Lorca, and a mutual friendship developed. De Falla's talent for creative artistic treatment of traditional folk themes in his music found parallel expression in some of Lorca's popular lyrics and especially in his poems of the *Cante jondo* (to be discussed later). During these years Lorca was also discovered by Don Fernando de los Ríos, an important leader in the movement toward the artistic, political and intellectual renovation of Spain. De los Ríos was important in convincing Lorca's father that Federico should transfer to the University of Madrid. This was a move keenly pleasing to him, since it meant wide freedom of action. He later managed to complete the requirements and received his law degree in 1923.

In 1918 García Lorca printed in Granada his first book, a prose work called *Impressions and Landscapes* (*Impresiones y paisajes*). A year earlier Lorca had formed part of a group of students which toured the important regions of Andalusia, Castile, Leon, and Galicia. Formerly, Azorín and Antonio Machado had written perceptively of Castile, Ramón del Valle-Inclán of Galicia. Following their examples, when Lorca returned from his journey, he assembled his notes and had the volume printed at his own expense. In this book Lorca first revealed a custom, to which both he and Juan Ramón Jiménez were addicted, that of having numerous volumes "in preparation." Lorca modestly promised six volumes, none of which ever appeared. He was thereafter to show a surprising carelessness with manuscripts, often leaving them unfinished, and unpublished even when finished. But when Lorca held his first book in his hands he knew that he had found his vocation in life.

As a work of literary art, *Impressions and Landscapes* has minor value, since the prose style shows immaturity and the book lacks originality of form, but it has importance in revealing the development of Lorca and in giving us a young man's reaction to certain features of Spanish life. In a style plagued with adjectives, overblown in the manner of Gustavo Adolfo Bécquer and impressionistic as in the mode of Juan Ramón Jiménez, the young Lorca records his deep feeling of melancholy as he describes the ancient buildings of Spain, especially the churches and monasteries. And in much of Spain he tends to see "a tragedy of contrasts . . . between mysticism and lust." Lorca, in his first book, shows a vivid imagination in a "nightmare" he sees stalking the streets near the Albaicín, "a figure eternally pregnant . . . [a] satanic hermaphrodite [showing the] greenish flesh of death . . . which would kiss us all to infect us with its evil." [3]

III *Lorca as The Student in Madrid*

It was in the spring of 1919 that Lorca arrived in Madrid and settled down in the famous *Residencia de Estudiantes,* living quarters for students who were attending the University and various professional schools in the city. The *Residencia,* which had been established around 1900 as part of a movement toward educational reform by men like Francisco Giner, offered arts and science training in the enlightened manner of European schools, especially the English. The atmosphere of the *Residencia* was generally one of seriousness and dedication; its aim was to educate young men for the responsibilities of leadership toward modernizing Spain. Conservative families naturally tended to regard it as a center of assorted heresies and excessive liberty. Famous figures associated with the *Residencia* earlier had been Menéndez Pidal, Unamuno, Antonio Machado, Juan Ramón Jiménez, Ortega y Gassett and Américo Castro. Thus there was room for surprising diversity in this free atmosphere. Menéndez Pidal, profound student of Spanish history, literature and language, was a staunch defender of Spanish tradition, while Ortega y Gassett soon became the strongest exponent and propagator of European ideas and innovations. Juan Ramón Jiménez, already conscious of his position as a great poet, occasionally visited the *Residencia* to encourage the fledgling poets.

García Lorca, after some initial difficulties caused perhaps by his provincialism, soon became acquainted with many promising young men who were residents or visitors and who later became prominent in Spanish letters, especially the members of the Generation of 1927: Rafael Alberti,[4] Jorge Guillén, Pedro Salinas, Gerardo Diego, Dámaso Alonso, Luis Cernuda, Vicente Aleixandre, and Manuel Atolaguirre. Lorca, who first made his mark in the *Residencia* when he sat down at the piano and began to improvise selections, soon began to exchange verses or to distribute them as gifts among the group. At this period Madrid was truly a hotbed of potential poetic talents. In time Lorca apparently became the leader of a smaller, more intimate group, including Pepín Bello, Salvador Dalí and Luis Buñuel, but none of the Generation of 1927. In the *Residencia* Lorca established a life pattern he was to continue for many years. Temperamentally unsuited to disciplined study, he and his group spent much time in the cafés, in witty discussion of vanguard literature and liberal social ideas, but he also consistently found time (nobody understood how) to write a great deal of poetry and to make a beginning in drama.

After his arrival in Madrid, Lorca made friends with Gregorio Martínez Sierra, the author of the famous *Cradle Song* (*Canción de Cuna*), and at that time a director of the Eslava Theater. Perhaps partly because of friendship, Martínez in early 1920 staged Lorca's first attempt at drama, *The Evildoing of the Butterfly* (*El maleficio de la mariposa*), a two-act piece in the manner of Maeterlinck or of Rostand's *Chantecler*. The improbable story concerns a little cockroach who is living acceptably with his family until one day a wounded butterfly is brought to his home. The cockroach soon aspires to the ideal world of the butterfly, and against the advice of friends he gives up the everyday world. But of course his idealistic world soon crashes when the butterfly rejects his advances. Then the little cockroach asks philosophically, "Who commands me to suffer without having wings?" The play has a full cast of unusual characters, including a gluttonous lizard. Apparently Lorca intended the play to be ingenuously poetic and idealistic, rather than ironic, but the delicate tone would be very difficult to sustain even with a select audience. Predictably, when the gluttonous lizard remarked, "Today I gobbled up nine flies," someone in the audience shouted indignantly, "How revolting!" Thus Lorca's first attempt in the theater was a failure, but he accepted it calmly.

In 1921, at the suggestion of a printer friend, Gabriel García Maroto, Lorca published a selection of his early lyrics, *Book of Poems* (*Libro de poemas*). While the earliest poem is dated 1915, the majority of them were composed in 1918–19, before Lorca had arrived in Madrid. Although one published notice was entitled "A New Poet," outside the circle of the *Residencia* the book aroused little excitement, and did little to create Lorca's poetic reputation.[5] One reason for the book's failure to arouse attention was its appearance at a moment when the vanguard ideas in poetry were gaining strength. The total effect of the book is weakened by its length—seventy-nine poems, many of them prolix and showing a lack of concentration. Of course various poems suggest themes utilized by the mature Lorca. For example, "Elegy," dedicated to the maternal and passionate Andalusian woman whom Lorca saw doomed usually to sterility, becomes a source of much of his drama.

Lorca's prologue to the book is correct: It is all the passion and torture of what he calls the memory of a "passionate infancy running nude among the meadows of the plain" of Granada. There are various themes: The clash between idealism and realism, the failure of passion against melancholic resignation, a concern with poetic expression itself, a concern with the questions of life after death, and a certain juvenile satanism. Over all there is a glow of melancholy and innocence which is not characteristic of Lorca's later work. A preoccupation with time indicates his reading of Antonio Machado, for example in the "Song of Spring" and "The Diamond." The music of "Ballad of a July Day" suggests Juan Ramón Jiménez. The fiercely erotic pieces sound like early Rubén Darío; the satanism is in the manner of Valle-Inclán. The anthologizers have correctly extracted one convincing lyric, the "Ballad of the Little Plaza," which is charming, musical, tenderly melancholy:

The children are singing,	(Cantan los niños
In the quiet night:	en la noche quieta:
Hushéd fountain,	¡ arroyo claro,
Streamlet bright!	fuente serena!)

During the years 1921–23, still usually in the atmosphere of the *Residencia,* Lorca devoted his basic energies to the development of his poetic talent, while still struggling against superficial distractions. In Madrid he began to soak up the new poetic direction generally called *ultraísmo* (to be discussed later), which was to find expression in his *Songs* (*Canciones*). At the same time he maintained close ties with his native Andalusia, especially through his friendship with Manuel de Falla. He gave evidence of growing maturity when he returned to Granada and conducted with de Falla a celebration of the *Deep Song* (*Cante jondo*). His own role was to deliver a lecture on the "Primitive Andalusian Song." But while in the *Residencia* he spent much time in student pranks. Later he recalled how he and other students set up a "Cabaña in the Desert" in his room, went days without going outside, then called for help from the astonished students.[6] Obviously Lorca and his group did not always conform to the serious atmosphere of the *Residencia*.

IV *Federico García Lorca and Salvador Dalí*

The years after the publication of *Book of Poems*, approximately 1924–28, were troubled years for Lorca, as his biography and his work reveal. There were moments of elation, followed by periods of deep depression. During this period his poetic genius developed, culminating in the publication of the *Gypsy Ballads* (*Romancero gitano*) in 1928. It is necessary at this point to trace the delicate and difficult story of Lorca's relations with Salvador Dalí, since the poet's subsequent writing bears some imprint of the story. Lorca, who often put personal references in his work, apparently remembered their first meeting in a poem: "The first time/I knew you not./The second, yes." Apparently their comradeship developed slowly in the first years while they were living in the close friendship of the *Residencia*.

As Dalí remembered later in *The Secret Life of Salvador Dalí*, Lorca produced an immense impression upon him. "The poetic phenomenon in its entirety . . . presented itself before me suddenly in flesh and bone, confused, blood-red, viscous and sublime, quivering with a thousand fires of darkness and of subterranean biology . . ."[7] By the time Dalí was settled in the *Residencia*, he insists that he and Lorca were the leaders of one of the subgroups, "The artistic-literary advance guard, a non-conformist group, strident and revolutionary."[8] According to Dalí, the group tended to assume an anti-intellectual color, to take to the cafés and express more openly its hostility to bourgeois mentality. Within the group the two budding geniuses immediately felt the mutual pressure of competition for leadership. Even Dalí admits Lorca won the first round, for when the fascinating Andalusian would "shine like a mad and fiery diamond" in the café literary sessions, Dalí would take off in a jealous rage and disappear for days.[9]

During his *Residencia* days Lorca had early set up the pattern of returning to Granada or a vacation place during the summer. In 1925 Salvador invited him to Catalonia to visit in the Dalí home. The family had a summer place in Cadaqués, in a location with an inspiring natural setting on the Costa Brava which enchanted Lorca. During this period he was becoming more intimate with Dalí, more impressed with his artistic talent and ideals and his personal attractiveness. He writes to a Catalonian friend, Sebastián Gasch: "In this boy, in my judgment, is the greatest glory of *eternal Catalonia*. I am preparing a study on him . . ." [10] In another letter: "I feel more each day the talent of Dalí . . . His extremely keen intelligence is united with a disconcerting infantilism . . . What moves me most in him now is his *delirium* of construction." And at the end of the same letter, there is a strangely passionate declaration: "Dalí moves me: he produces in me the same pure emotion (and may God Our Father pardon me) produced in me by the child Jesus, abandoned in the Portal of Bethlehem, with the germ of the Crucifixion already latent in the straw of the cradle." [11]

At this time Lorca was entering a period of intense emotional excitement. On arriving in Cadaqués he immediately brought under his spell the Dalí family. He soon assembled the family group, especially the elder Dalí and Ana María, the daughter, and read to them *Mariana Pineda*. All his contemporaries insist that Lorca was a spell-binding reader, particularly when he read his own work; the traditionalist Dalí family was overwhelmed by the emotion of the play, and little by little began to treat Lorca like one of the family. Ana María's book on her brother Salvador, written much later, seems to indicate that Lorca was suffering from serious emotional problems. [12] The family was unaware of Lorca's personal involvement with Salvador, nor did they even suspect the latter's total rebellion against Christian values, a rebellion that was later to shatter the Dalí family. But Ana María perceived that Lorca was under serious emotional strain, with signs of hypochondria. Lorca begged to be watched over, complained of all sorts of illnesses, was obsessed by death, was inordinately frightened of entering the water. She specifically remembered that Lorca was preoccupied with attending Mass, reacted to the service with unusual emotion and seemed to be able to achieve serenity in no other place. This testimony is surprising when we recall how generally the Spanish literary figures of the twentieth century have been anti-Church, especially in the practice of Catholic observances.

In that summer of 1925, or soon after he left Cadaqués, Lorca wrote in classic unrhymed Alexandrines (a sixteen syllable line) an "Ode to Salvador Dalí" ("Oda a Salvador Dalí"), which José Ortega y Gassett printed in the important *Revista de Occidente* of April, 1926. The ode and its publication is Lorca's first but prime example of poetic arrogance. If we remember that in 1925 Dalí was exactly 21, that he was known as an eccentric prankster in Madrid, that he had painted nothing at all of value by 1925, surely someone must have been puzzled by Lorca's use of a pretentious literary form like the ode in such circumstances. Moreover, Lorca forces the reader to interpret it basically as a love poem. In the first part he analyzes Dalí's painting technique for the coming years, involving Freudian dream images painted with classic detail and no abstraction. But he then says that he is not praising Dalí's imperfect adolescent brush and goes on to this conclusion, which indicates the turbulence of their mutual attraction:

> But above all else I sing a common thought
> That makes us one in dark and golden hours.
> It is not Art the light that blinds our eyes.
> It is love first, friendship or fencing match.

> (Pero ante todo canto un común pensamiento
> que nos une en las horas oscuras y doradas.
> No es el Arte la luz que nos ciega los ojos.
> Es primero el amor, la amistad o la esgrima.)

In 1926, Lorca suddenly approached what were for him new ideas. Apparently he finally realized that he could not continue forever to live totally off his parents. To the poet Guillén, who represented the link between Lorca's world and society, he declared that he was going to prepare himself for a professorship in literature.[13] (Guillén, Unamuno, Machado, Salinas were all professors.) Strangely, since he had long been a student and should have known, he asked Guillén how to begin. Then he immediately wrote Guillén again, this time introducing the idea that perhaps he would like to marry and settle down, but then admitted in the next line that he never could.[14] Lorca soon forgot both professorship and marriage, and we wonder if there is not a sense of desperation in the situation. Apparently his family had begun to exert pressure upon him to marry and settle down.

The influence of Dalí, both personal and artistic, continued to increase. Vázquez Ocaña insists that the Catalán, by proximity to the border of France, was able to follow the most revolutionary of the new aesthetic currents from that country.[16] It is certain that at that time Dalí was the one who was able more easily to reject violently the whole weight of his Catholic tradition. With his fantastic and cultivated mania toward self-absorption, every phase of even his bodily processes fascinated him; therefore in the early 1920's when he had begun to study Freud's *Interpretation of Dreams,* Dalí confessed that it was one of the "capital discoveries" of his life.[16] He began to concentrate on unusual biological processes, the total range of sexual aspects and on the ramifications of his own genius. The Freudian ideas, which of course permeated the very air in this decade, for Dalí and Lorca came to mean freedom from the restraints of their conservative Catholic and family traditions.[17]

Lorca returned to Cadaqués in the summer of 1927. He and Dalí then went to Barcelona, where they arranged a showing of the former's drawings. Obviously Dalí is now influencing Lorca. These drawings, some of which are reproduced in the *Obras completas,* are representational line drawings whose meaning is often very clear. For example, Vázquez Ocaña describes "Amor novo" as a "muscular sailor with long feminine lashes surging from a tombstone with a moon in the background." [18] But apparently at this very time Lorca realized that his relationship with Dalí could not endure. Having returned to Granada, he writes to his friend Gasch: "My spiritual state is not very good . . . I am passing through a great 'crisis of love (*sentimiento*)' from which I hope to emerge cured." [19]

In this turbulent year of 1927 Lorca clearly revealed his marvelous energy and talent for concentration. In January he published some prose selections; in April a book of poems, *Songs (Canciones)*; in July some of the *Gypsy Ballads;* in April his study of Soto de Rojas; in December, a prose selection in the *Revista de Occidente.* In the summer he was working on a tragedy, *The Sacrifice of Iphigenia (El sacrificio de Iphigenia)*, a manuscript later lost or destroyed. He helped to organize the showing of his drawings in Barcelona in June. In June he saw the opening of his play *Mariana Pineda* in Barcelona, and a second opening in Madrid in October. In October he initiated plans for a journal, *Cock* (*Gallo*), he was to edit. In December he attended a literary conference in Seville, and read his important essay, "The Poetic Image in don Luis de Góngora."

The year 1928 was for García Lorca one of artistic triumph. In this year he finally collected the poems of the *Gypsy Ballads* in the book which was to bring him international fame. He had begun the ballads in 1924, a few of them had been printed in periodicals, and some were well-known in his circle from his personal readings. The enthusiastic reception of the book seemingly should have sustained him. By the time of the publication of the *Book of Poems* he was sure of what he wanted to be. But as he read the published *Gypsy Ballads* and observed the enthusiastic critical reception of the book, he was finally certain that he would be a major poet, and his preference for the *Ballads* never wavered.

But 1928 was also for Lorca the year of a personal tragedy. His relations with Dalí came to an end, and from later writings we can comprehend the seriousness of the attachment for both Lorca and Dalí. Dalí, looking back almost twenty years later, is for him surprisingly reticent. He admits in his autobiography that Lorca overwhelmed him initially, but that gradually he successfully resisted. In a concluding passage Dalí, though not yet ready to unveil the story completely, reveals that in this period the "shadow of Maldoror" hung over his life; he must be referring to the end of Lautréamont's *Chants of Maldoror* (*Chants de Maldoror*), where an older Maldoror lays siege against a young man in his own house, and finally succeeds in enticing him away from his family. And then Dalí adds that at that period "Federico García Lorca . . . came and darkened the virginal originality of my spirit and my flesh." [20]

Lorca reveals a new state of mind in various letters to his friend Jorge Zalamea, and in two isolated poems[21] apart from his books of poetry. To Zalamea he writes, "I am a little against everyone, but the live beauty that pulses in my hands comforts me . . . And having conflicts of a very grave sentiment and being *overcome* with love, with society, with other things, I have and continue my norm of joy at all costs . . ."[22] After trying to encour-

[29]

age Zalamea, who apparently has problems himself, Lorca goes on: "I have *resolved* these days by will power one of the most painful states I have had in my life." And in another letter he puts his situation on a moral plane: "One needs to have the sum of joy that God has given me not to succumb before the conflicts which have recently assaulted me. But God never abandons me." [23]

This manner of expression conditions us to accept the strong expression of the "Ode to the Most Holy Sacrament of the Altar," written in this period. In the first part of the poem Lorca evokes a Christ suffering almost beyond description; then he brings Him down to the greatest intimacy with man, making Him a "sweet cake for the newborn." The agony of the poet's need is entirely convincing; not even Unamuno surpassed the expression of poignant need in this "Ode." Then, in a second section, "World," the poet seems near suicide. But the final line sets up a permanent point of reference and a course of action for the poet: "Immutable Sacrament of love and discipline!"

It was during this same year (1928) that Lorca launched his first literary project, and with his usual enthusiasm. From his native Granada Lorca succeeded in founding *Cock* (*Gallo*) as a supplement of the Granada newspaper. He immediately began to plague his friends for material. Initially his plan was to encourage unknown local talent (his brother Francisco for one); soon, however, he began to envision more broadly a great magazine with Andalusian talent to compete with that of Madrid. He also projected, mostly for personal reasons, a voice that would join Andalusia with Catalonia; before printing two numbers he was contemplating a whole number on Dalí, who of course still hardly merited such an honor.

Lorca and his group, including various Catalonian men of letters such as Gasch and Dalí, succeeded in publishing two numbers, both of which caused a scandal in provincial Granada. In the first number Lorca himself wrote a "History of This *Cock*," a delightfully imaginative piece with his usual symbolic intent. It is quite incredible how Lorca included so much of the personal history of himself and his group, all in the vaguest suggestion of course, while at the same time constructing an ingenious program for the journal which would satisfy the *putrefied ones*. The second issue really shocked provincial Granada, since it contained the

"Catalonian Anti-artistic Manifesto" by Dalí, and two obscure, vanguard, semi-Freudian pieces by Lorca. For various reasons—lack of public support, narrow aims, and perhaps the personal problems of Lorca—*Gallo* failed to appear again after two issues.

After the expense of creating his poems of passion and moral conflict, Lorca suffered what Vázquez Ocaña calls another of his "strange periodical crises." [24] Since around 1926 he had been vacillating between attraction to and rejection of Dalí and the revolutionary world he represented. But now in 1928 he chose to break away completely from Dalí and their circle. Already he had confided to Guillén that he had a sharp desire to get away from Spain, preferably to go to Paris, where he could write the kind of poems prohibited in Spain. [25] And so, just before he left Granada in 1929, in a few moving words he summed up his struggle at the moment: "Now more than ever I need silence . . . to sustain the duel to the death that I am sustaining with my heart and with poetry. With my heart, to free it from the impossible passion that destroys . . . With poetry, to construct, in spite of her who defends herself like a virgin, a living and true poem where beauty and horror and the ineffable and the repugnant live and clash together . . . in the midst of candent joy." [26] Lorca in his honest but poetic way had just told an audience at a lecture of his struggle with Dalí. According to Schonberg, his family was crushed when the situation was revealed, his father threatening never to see him again. The time he seized the opportunity to accompany his old friend Fernando de los Ríos on a brief trip to Paris and London, with the final destination New York.

V *Interlude in New York*

In the early summer of 1929 Lorca, after a brief visit in Paris and London, arrived in New York, to be greeted by Angel del Río, for many years a professor at Columbia University. Lorca settled in John Hay Hall and registered as a student in classes of English for foreigners. Even before leaving Spain Lorca was keenly aware of the incongruity of his going to New York, and it soon became obvious that English would remain a mystery to him.

After a very little time Lorca escaped into a vacation in Vermont in the home of a friend, Philip Cummings, a young man who had been studying in Spain. Lorca seems to have been in a dangerous psychological state, for Cummings reported later that he repeatedly expressed hostility toward his family. Apparently his father had encouraged him to make the trip with the hope that he would regain his equilibrium.

While in the quiet atmosphere of rural Vermont, Lorca began to write some of the poems of *Poet in New York* (*Poeta en Nueva York*). The poems indicate how strange Lorca found this environment compared to that of his student days in Madrid. It is interesting that almost all the poems began with a concrete experience, which he transmuted into abstract and symbolic poetry.

When Lorca returned to New York he seems to have recovered some of his former energy. He began to renew friendships with various Spaniards in New York and to make new ones among the Spanish literary group. Dámaso Alonso was teaching that year at Hunter College. During the year he met the bullfighter Ignacio Sánchez Mejías, later immortalized in Lorca's elegy, the guitarist Andrés Segovia, the dancer La Argentinita. Federico de Onís and León Felipe were also in New York as professors. Among the Americans interested in Spanish he became friends with Herschell Brickell and with Mildred Adams, translator of Ortega y Gassett. He attended many parties, and even though his English was extremely limited, he was still able to dominate a group with his ability at the piano and his folksongs.

The two aspects of Lorca's personality were much in evidence in New York. The Lorca of social magnetism created a strong impression in the dormitory at Columbia where he lived. Professor John Crow, who roomed near him that year, has reported how Lorca entertained the group with imaginative experiences, especially some relating to poems in the *Gypsy Ballads*. Crow admits to being taken aback at times by Lorca's excessive self-confidence. But Crow also reveals that Lorca "spent late hours in many a Harlem dive, [and] walked Brooklyn Bridge at midnight"—not with the Columbia group.[27] It is this Lorca, suffering from alienation, who wrote the poems of *Poet in New York*. Professor Crow, who was not prepared to accept this alienated, rebellious Lorca, concluded that the book was not characteristic of his work.

During the year, in addition to the poems of *Poet in New York*, Lorca wrote much of the full-length farce, *The Shoemaker's Prodigious Wife* (*La zapatera prodigiosa*), and apparently a first version of *Yerma*. He also found time to work on two of his surrealist pieces, *Thus Five Years Pass* (*Así que pasen cinco años*) and *The Public* (*El público*). He gave lectures at Vassar on "Imagination, Inspiration and Evasion in Poetry," a repeat of one given in Madrid, and on "Cradle Songs." Apparently he also began to study Walt Whitman in translation, with the encouragement of León Felipe, one of the American poet's early translators. Even in this period of stress, and agitated by an unfamiliar environment, Lorca continued to create original work. However, he made little attempt to participate in contemporary American literary activity during his stay.

In the spring of 1930, having received an invitation to give some lectures in Cuba, Lorca set sail for Havana and a culture at least partly like his own. On arriving, he was received warmly by Nicolás Guillén and Emilio Ballagas. Lorca, as the supposed hero of the Spanish gypsies, found a brotherhood among these poets, at the moment exploiting phases of the primitive Negro themes of Cuba. With his talent for assimilating modes of expression, Lorca cast one of the final poems of *Poet in New York* in one of the Cuban popular forms. Apparently he delivered four lectures, the important one being "Theory and Function of the Daemon." Deeply impressed by his reception and his reputation in a country which spoke his language, Lorca later remembered how strongly he felt pride in being a Spaniard and in the responsibility which this entailed.

VI Years of Glory in a World of Turmoil

When Lorca returned to Spain in late 1930, he encountered a tense political situation, but after a brief stay in Granada, he entered a teeming Madrid, apparently anxious to pursue his ideas of conquering the theater. In that year came the fall of the Rivera dictatorship and the creation of a new Republic, and everyone felt the seething political tension. Lorca's introduction to physical strife came as he was almost trampled when the Civil Guard dissolved a demonstration. He was quite frightened, and remained so afterward; the bloody aggression of the *Gypsy Ballads* is entirely poetic. Lorca, who of course had sympathy for the persecuted and a desire for social justice, nevertheless refused to employ his talents in any direct way to help either side in the

[33]

political struggle. In this whole matter, inevitably there arises the comparison with Rafael Alberti, also a poet of great talent, who joined the movement toward democratic freedom as he understood it for Spain.

The presentation of *The Shoemaker's Prodigious Wife* in late 1930, with Margarita Xirgu in the leading role, was a stunning triumph, a fine beginning for the new period in Lorca's life when the emphasis in his work shifts from the lyric to the dramatic. At this time he still felt the pull of two opposing currents in the drama. While *The Shoemaker's Prodigious Wife* is generally traditional, Lorca had also finished *Thus Five Years Pass* and *The Public,* two plays in the surrealist manner. Therefore it is fortunate for his dramatic development that he had the opportunity to explore the classic Spanish tradition.

In 1932 the Spanish republic created its Cultural Missions, of which there were two groups. Alejandro Casona, later to become a famous playwright, was named director of one group, García Lorca and Eduardo Ugarte, another young playwright, directors of the other, called the University Theater, and popularly known as La Barraca. The mission of this group was to employ university students as a theatrical company to carry theater into the provinces. The group of budding actors, after preparing a repertoire in Madrid, traveled across the provinces in a truck loaded with their own stage properties.

Lorca was of course ecstatic at the opportunity to work out some of the many ideas and plans always in his mind, and he soon became one of the moving spirits of the whole enterprise. Initially the group concentrated on plays from the classic Spanish theater, that is, mainly from the seventeenth century, Spain's Golden Age in literature. Lorca had always been interested in Lope de Vega, but now he had the opportunity and challenge of working with his plays with a real audience. Interestingly, the group first chose Lope's *Fuenteovejuna* (*The Sheep's Well*), a play with social overtones. But *La Barraca* also prepared Calderón's *Life is a Dream* (*La Vida es sueño*) and the universally popular *El burlador de Sevilla* (*The Seducer of Seville*) of Tirso de Molina. Since, like *Hamlet,* most of these plays ran long in the original, Lorca inherited the task of compressing scenes by the judicious removal of lines. His respect for the classic playwrights was so great that he refused to summarize scenes in his own verse. The group apparently presented little modern drama, and none of Lorca's, but it at least began its goal of education by presenting such little-known works as the eight *Entremeses* (*Interludes*) of Cervantes. What interested Lorca profoundly was the hunger of the people in the provinces for meaningful drama. Certainly his stimulus toward renovating the Spanish theater came in part from these experiences as a traveling play-producer.

Even while working with *La Barraca* Lorca continued to write original plays, and by the end of 1934 he began to devote less time to his directorship in order to concentrate on his own work. In March of 1933, *Blood Wedding* (*Bodas de sangre*) was staged for the first time in a commercial theater in Madrid. In April, a theater group presented his *Love of Don Perlimplín* (*Amor de Don Perlimplín*). Both public and critics were ready to admit that Lorca was now important in the Spanish theater, and plans were soon initiated to translate and stage *Blood Wedding* in France and the United States.

Late in 1933 Lorca made a long and triumphant journey to Buenos Aires. Three of his successful plays were staged, including a presentation of *Blood Wedding* with Lola Membrives in the leading role. Lorca himself directed a presentation of Lope de Vega's *The Silly Lady* (*La dama boba*), revised earlier for *La Barraca*. He also gave five lectures from his major critical essays, including "The Poetic Image in Don Luis de Góngora." During the summer of 1933, Lorca finished his revision of *Yerma* and saw it staged in December at the Spanish Theater in Madrid, where the play had a long run. In late 1935 he completed and staged *Doña Rosita the Spinster* (*Doña Rosita la soltera*) in Barcelona, and while the performance was a critical success, the play somehow became embroiled in politics.

During this period when his stature as a public figure was growing (1931–35), Lorca's private life is best reflected in a book-length diary published later by Carlos Morla, consul from Chile in Madrid.[28] Since Morla edited his journal specifically to include materials relating to Lorca, it seems as if he almost lived in Morla's home, a center for literary and cultural gatherings, but his heavy social activity and his continued writing again indicate his limitless energy. Lorca's long private discussions with Morla reveal that in spite of the encouragement of public approbation the real Lorca was suffering keenly from personal alienation, from feeling himself an outsider. But at times he was gay, charming and playful, a stimulating figure in a social gathering.

Morla's home was often the meeting place of a group of young artistic and cultural figures, among them Luis Cernuda, Rafael Martínez and the Chilean poet Pablo Neruda. Lorca and Neruda, the two important poets, had joined together during Lorca's visit to Argentina to pay homage to Rubén Darío. With Lorca as the acknowledged leader, the group often attended theatrical performances (sometimes Lorca's own) and various cultural gatherings, returning to Morla's home. Customarily, what Morla called the intimate group would remain after the others had left and discuss literature and life until the early hours of the morning. Lorca used Morla's salon as a sounding board for his work, often reading full-length plays to the assembled group; and while the response was usually overwhelming, the group's enthusiastic encouragement was of little critical help. Since several of the group were poets, Lorca sometimes seemed happy, but by 1935 he became discontented with this atmosphere and threatened to return to Granada.

During the years of *La Barraca* García Lorca lived through another serious emotional experience, the details of which were made public much later by Cipriano Rivas Cherif. Rivas, a well-known director in the theater, was with Lorca and Margarita Xirgu the actress in Barcelona for the opening of one of Lorca's plays. At a crucial time when Lorca failed to appear, Rivas went in search and finally found him in a café, in a seriously dejected mood. He began to pour out to the surprised Rivas the following story: A young fellow of little cultural background, the son of a laborer, had read Lorca's *Gypsy Ballads* and had sought acquaintance with Lorca. Lorca soon brought the lad under his influence, and to Rivas he showed and commented upon a series of letters which traced the progress of their mutual attachment. Lorca then had wangled a position for the young man in *La Barraca*. What had precipitated Lorca's crisis was that the lad had suddenly run off with an ordinary gypsy girl. The young man, identified by Rivas only as R., apparently was killed fighting in the Civil War.[29] Since Lorca went on to confess extremely important details about his attitudes toward life, this article is of supreme importance in interpreting the mature Lorca's work. He stated clearly his permanent rejection of the feminine, his refusal to accept marriage and the family as the only viable social system, and his support of some kind of exclusive personal and artistic comradeship among men, a system he thought to be Whitman's.[30]

Around 1936, in spite of the political tensions, García Lorca's mind as usual teemed with new plans and crystalizing ideas, and a sketch of these plans will indicate the continuing duality of his outlook on life. On the one hand, he was still in personal rebellion against important phases of Spanish Catholic culture. In addition to the poems of the *Divan of Tamarit* (*Diván del Tamarit*), Lorca had assembled a collection of about forty poems called the *Sonnets of Dark Love* (*Sonetos del amor oscuro*). In these sonnets Lorca was apparently attempting to defend (or project) a system of intimate masculine comradeship, whose roots he traced back to a new kind of Adam. He also claimed to have ready for publication a collection of three hundred poems to be entitled grimly *Introduction to Death* (*Introducción a la muerte*). He was also planning dramas with themes thus far forbidden in Madrid. *The Destruction of Sodom* (*La destrucción de Sodoma*) was almost finished. *Blood Has No Voice* (*La sangre no tiene voz*) was to be a modern, realistic version of the incest of Thamar and Amnon, which had been treated by Tirso de Molina in the Golden Age. Finally, he planned another to be called *Blackballed* (*La bola negra*), the tragedy of a homosexual in conflict with society. Obviously Lorca had conceived works of daring themes which dramatists such as Tennessee Williams later exploited successfully.

On the other hand, García Lorca was developing a genuine and mature concern for his people, was beginning to be able to approach dramatic problems objectively, and spiritually was struggling to make that return to the Catholic tradition which Rubén Darío had made before him. Before 1930 he and Dalí had both been intensely preoccupied with personal concerns. His interest in the gypsy and the Negro in New York had not been social concern; he had manipulated them as a metaphor. By 1935, however, he gave evidence of his growing social concern in plans for a new play, treating of religious and socioeconomic problems, and his explanation of it shows he is caught up in the ideas of the socialist upheavals of the 1930's. Certainly in plays of social import he could strive for objectivity in developing characters and themes. His last play, *The House of Bernarda Alba* (*La casa de Bernarda Alba*), which he never saw staged, is generally free of the personal symbols and preoccupations of its author.

In spirit, Lorca was also returning to the eternal Spanish tradition. He had plans to give lectures on Quevedo, whom he had recently rediscovered. Quevedo, ironic, satiric, profound, had lived through the declining years of the Golden Age. "Quevedo is Spain," said Lorca, and his concern with Quevedo's struggle with the tragic sense of life indicates that he was maturing rapidly. He had previously been playing with death; now he was preparing to struggle with it face to face, like Unamuno. There is a revealing discussion that Lorca had with the caricaturist Bagaría in 1936. Bagaría, tormented by a lack of faith, is pressing Lorca for assurance. And Lorca, in words reminiscent of Rubén Darío, declares simply, "I want to be good." [31] True to his Spanish heritage, he offers little hope of optimism in life, but he invokes the doctrine of the Church by remembering an epitaph seen in a ruined cemetery: "Here lies Doña Micaela Gómez, awaiting the resurrection of the flesh."

VII *Death in His Granada*

In a rapidly worsening political situation García Lorca apparently planned to retire to provincial Granada until the storms blew over in Madrid. He departed from Madrid on July 16, 1936, to return to his home and family. He had turned down an opportunity to evade danger by going to New York with Angel del Río, saying, "I'm a poet, and no one kills poets."

Of course he could not foresee the period of unbridled violence which had been threatening for years. From its inception in 1931, the course of the Second Republic had been marked by revolutionary strikes, anti-clerical outrages, and revolts against the government from both Left and Right. In 1931–33 the Left-Wing group in power, composed of trade unions, socialists, and many intellectuals, passed laws dealing with agrarian reform, regional autonomy and the forbidding of the religious orders to teach. In 1933–35 the Center-Right group in power, composed of the landed aristocracy, Church and Army, reversed the direction of the former government and passed a new agrarian law benefitting landowners, postponed the replacing of religious with lay schools and violently suppressed revolts in Barcelona and especially in Asturias in October, 1934. In 1936, the Popular Front, generally Leftist, came back to power, but the fact that persistent general strikes occurred and that many churches were burned during a four-month period indicates the political chaos. On July 17 the Army in Morocco, led by General Franco, revolted against the Spanish government, and within days the whole country was in civil war. Very soon both sides lost most of their sense of human justice and began reprisals and counter-reprisals among the people, since of course the two opposing groups were not geographically separated.

Lorca arrived in Granada while the Nationalist forces of the Army were subduing the Popular forces in fierce fighting. The Army forces in Granada then began a purge of socialists, liberal intellectuals and union leaders. One of the early victims was the socialist mayor of Granada, Fernández Montesinos, husband of Lorca's sister Concha. The bands of "Black Squads" began their rounds, the sound of their trucks carrying victims to firing squads filling everyone with terror. Lorca as an intellectual with popular sympathies knew he was under suspicion. His family in desperation finally persuaded him to seek refuge in the house of a friend, the poet Luis Rosales, whose brothers were powerful in the Falange, the fascist group, which had recently been organized to preserve traditional Spanish institutions. With the Rosales temporarily absent from the house, Lorca was arrested by a squad, spent a night in captivity in Granada, and on the morning of August 19 was taken to a place outside Granada called Viznar and shot. He was buried there in a ravine along with many others.

In spite of the savagery of the Civil War, García Lorca was, perhaps surprisingly, the only major literary figure killed directly in it. The reaction to his death among cultured groups of Spain and of all Europe and America was one of shocked horror. Since 1936 there has been intense effort to search out every detail in order to fix the responsibility for his death. Various stories have been advanced. After a long silence, the Falange insisted that Ruiz Alonso, a deputy of the Catholic Party, had ordered Lorca's death in reprisal when a false rumor arose that the Republicans had shot the dramatist Jacinto Benavente.[32] Schonberg tries to prove the story (which had long been rumor) that Lorca was killed during the general upheaval in a personal vendetta by a group of homosexuals he had made enemies of in Granada.[33] Whether or not it was because the poet soon became a symbol for the defeated Republican side the Clerical and Falange groups refused to accept official blame for the deed. With much bad faith on both sides, of course no totally acceptable account has emerged, though there is an idea that in Granada many people know the true story.

The death of Federico García Lorca was a senseless tragedy, and we refrain from pursuing the political controversies which have utilized his name. After the deed, a great wrath emanated from Spain and Spanish America; the writers have fulminated against the easy enemy, the guilty "they," declaring Lorca's innocence. Then, if we accept his innocence, which of the one million Spaniards who perished in the Civil War were "guilty"? If it is meaningless to blame him for helping to cause the war with his revolutionary attitudes as a poet, it is equally meaningless to praise him for anything, since he had consistently turned his back on the increasing political intransigence in his country, not trying either to comprehend or to exercise influence. This statement attributed to Pemán, which means everything and nothing, exemplifies the futility of grandiose pronouncements: "The death of Lorca at the hands of unknown persons was a crime against Spain." [34] For us, the rest is an almost unbearable silence.

CHAPTER 2

Lorca's Poetic Formation and Early Poetry

I Lorca's Poetic Formation

IN order to comprehend Lorca's poetic formation, we must discuss briefly the literary movements in force during his formative years, especially the international vanguard movements ultraism and surrealism, and his critical reaction to them.[1] When Lorca arrived in Madrid, he had written most of his *Book of Poems,* which reveals the influence of poets like Valle-Inclán and Darío, and the more general influence of the early poetry of Juan Ramón Jiménez and Antonio Machado. Jiménez, who had begun to write around 1900 in the manner of the French impressionists and with the polished and sonorous forms of Darío, gradually began to strive for a pure poetry of sparse form, serene beauty and eternal symbol. By 1916, on the strength of books such as *Diary of a Poet Recently Married (Diario de un poeta reciéncasado)* he had established himself as perhaps the outstanding Spanish poet. He shared this role with Machado, whose *Solitudes (Soledades)* and *Land of Castile (Campos de Castilla),* 1912, had consolidated his reputation as a major poet of the Generation of 1898. But by 1919 some younger poets such as Gerardo Diego and Guillermo de Torre began to feel that both Jiménez and Machado were too traditional to exert decisive influence on the ultraistic movement.[2] In journals such as *Grecia* (1919) and *Ultra* (1921) they attempted to define and provide outstanding examples of ultraism.

The literary movement called ultraism in Spain was developed under influences of a similar vanguard movement in France, its chief exponent there being Pierre Reverdy, according to Torre.[3] The ultraistic poets set as a goal the renovation of the image and the metaphor, looking toward a synthesis of the two. The ultraistic metaphor involved a leap, a sudden illumination, an evasion of reality, a stylized word-play. The *created* poems were to be just that, a *creation*, independent of the world or reality. These poets usually rejected rhyme and auditive suggestion, but stressed a visible architecture (without punctuation) on the page—a technique clearly adapted from the French poet Mallarmé. Torre stressed the fact that in addition the poets sought to develop a new poetic structure, but this ideal remained largely unrealized; for while many brilliant images and metaphors burst forth, the poems were often a series of insufficiently related metaphors. In some ways, two Spaniards had already been struggling toward this new direction. Ramón Gómez de la Serna in his *greguerías*, a kind of poetic aphroism, was very close to a new type of metaphor, and we have already mentioned Valle-Inclán's creation of the *esperpento* manner, in which there is a deformation of reality. From this period, Gerardo Diego's *Image* (*Imagen*), written before 1921, and Guillermo de Torre's *Propellers* (*Hélices*) are the most typical books of poetry of the movement. José Ortega y Gassett later analyzed the theory of the movement in his essay, "The Dehumanization of Art." García Lorca, who was absorbing ultraism without declaring himself a proponent, assimilated many of its doctrines in his book *Songs* (*Canciones*), written in 1921–24. It is of course not clear whether Lorca followed Diego directly or whether the two were influenced by a common source.

Undoubtedly of more importance in Lorca's poetic formation was the influence of surrealism, which appeared as a movement with André Bretón's *Manifesto* of 1924. Bretón defined the practice of surrealism as the poet's surrendering himself to pure automatism; in this state the conscious tries to free itself of all logical control and all aesthetic and moral preoccupation, with an attempt to tap the sources of the unconscious. Attempting to utilize this manner as a source of inspiration inevitably invokes Freud's *Interpretation of Dreams* and related works of psychology. For as Freud tells us, the images evoked in some kind of dream state are primitive or basic, and often connected with bodily processes, especially the sexual. The surrealists found excellent literary models in Lautréamont's *Chants of Maldoror* and Rimbaud's *A Season in Hell* (*Une saison en Enfer*). Since the French surrealists were often viciously anti-social, anti-religious and tended toward utter frankness of expression, most of the Spanish poets influenced by surrealism, Alberti and Aleixandre for example, proved to be unwilling to subscribe to such extremes. But for García Lorca surrealism appeared at a critical moment during his years of association with Dalí, when both were ripe for rebellion. Dalí, who embraced surrealism joyfully and totally, later in the 1930's gave it outstanding expression in his painting. His "Family of Marsupial Centaurs" is an evocation so perfectly Freudian as to seem a travesty, but Dalí consistently demonstrated the talent for dredging up images to turn any surrealist green with envy. Lorca soon revealed a talent for images comparable to Dalí's, and for a number of years they tended to share a personal symbolism.

Lorca certainly utilized the surrealist manner, first in his odes around 1926, and in certain of the *Gypsy Ballads,* such as the "Somnambulistic Ballad." We must note that Lorca declared that he never quite surrendered to the unconscious, and even his surrealist poems have "poetic logic." [4] In actual fact, since by definition the unconscious remains inaccessible to the conscious mind, no one can utilize the unconscious deliberately, but the poets have been able to work with the symbols of the unconscious. What Lorca meant by "poetic logic" seems to be that whereas some surrealists tended to utter massive incoherence, his surrealist poems generally have a consistent thematic development. The outstanding feature of his surrealist poems is that they seem to have come from a dream-state. Perhaps Lorca's most obvious example is a poem called "The Siren and the Carabineer" (1927), couched in the Spanish Alexandrines. While a complete analysis of the poem would require pages, briefly it is a song of mariners, singing "songs of bamboo" with "refrains of snow." Cocks and dolphins play around broken bridges, while "equivocated maps" (bodies) gleam in the mariners' eyes. Meanwhile night, disguised with a mule hide (repression), is pushing away the "Latin barks," a symbol of Catholic moral tradition. This poem is extremely difficult, but we think Lorca was projecting a veiled homosexual phantasy. After various experiments of this type, Lorca wrote almost all the *Poet in New York* in this manner, and as a book it is probably the outstanding example of surrealism in Spanish literature.

But as we have indicated before, in his artistic formation Lorca persisted in assimilating the vanguard while at the same time penetrating into the traditional. The reputation and the steady performance of the older and more traditional poets Jiménez, Antonio Machado and Unamuno served as a brake for his iconoclastic tendencies. Moreover, Antonio Machado and his brother Manuel, along with Salvador Rueda, had led the way to an exploitation of Andalusian folklore. Lorca, with an additional stimulus from Manuel de Falla, by 1921 had begun his poems of the *Deep Song* (*Cante jondo*), his first important poetry. Apparently, however, Lorca was so strongly impressed by the artistic vanguard that he delayed in printing these poems and proceeded to blend the traditional and the vanguard in his *Gypsy Ballads.*

With the ultraistic movements wildly stressing the extravagant image and metaphor, art as elegant play, and similar anti-realistic doctrines, it was inevitable that the tradition-oriented and yet novelty-seeking Spaniards would rediscover Don Luis de Góngora, one of the outstanding Baroque poets in European literature. Góngora had it all: recondite metaphor, aristocratic elegance, art as art, but couched in traditional form and within traditional social and religious philosophies. The return to Góngora, heralded by Rubén Darío, is given expression by Torre as a precursor of the ultraistic manner in 1925. The apotheosis of this return occurred in 1927, when the most important of the young poets gathered in Seville to honor him on the three-hundredth anniversary of his death.

At this time Lorca made his first critical venture with "The Poetic Image in Don Luis de Góngora," presented in Granada as a lecture in 1927, in which he was able to bring together the traditional and the vanguard by finding in Góngora the salient qualities of the ultraistic poetry. According to Lorca, Góngora invents for the first time in Spanish "a new method for hunting and shaping metaphors, and thinks, without saying it, that the eternity of a poem depends on the quality and structure of its images." And at times Góngora doubles and triples the image in order to communicate multiple sensations on different planes of meaning. And what of the "obscurity" in Góngora? Lorca insists that in fact Góngora sins by being too luminous. Undoubtedly making a plea for his own generation, which tended to be hermetic, Lorca declares that Góngora is not to be merely read, that to understand him one must cultivate adequate sensibility to poetry. And what of the aristocratic and popular in Góngora? Lorca, surely speaking for himself also, holds that in Góngora the image is always aristocratic. Góngora, like all great poets, has a poetic world apart, in which an apple is as important as the ocean. In his essay Lorca proved, as did the other poets of his generation, that he could practice and defend the basic elements of ultraistic poetry without going outside the Spanish poetic tradition.

Another essay important to Lorca's literary formation is his "Theory and Function of the Daemon" ("Teoría y juego del duende"), given as a lecture in Cuba in 1930, after he had weathered his most intense personal crisis and after the publication of the *Gypsy Ballads* had assured his poetic reputation. In the essay he is searching for the sources of poetic inspiration. In ascending scale they are three: the muse, the angel and the duende, or daemon. This daemon, in the "ultimate habitations" of the blood, is a power that begins in the soles of the feet and courses through the body to the throat of the artist. Not intelligence or form, the daemon is a power which appears when there is communication with God through the five senses; above all the daemon never appears unless there is at least the possibility of death.

In the essay Lorca discusses a diverse group of artists who have known the daemon. First, there was Socrates, who, we remember, was forced to drink the hemlock because he corrupted the youth of Athens; and there was Descartes, who, "tired of circles and lines, went down to the canals to listen to the drunken sailors." In his list Lorca includes Quevedo, Jorge Manrique, el Greco and Goya, Rimbaud and Lautréamont, an extensive group of Flamenco singers and dancers, bullfighters like Belmonte and Joselito, and in this increasingly strange company, St. Teresa and St. John of the Cross. Jorge Guillén thought Lorca not serious when he insisted on picking out three little-discussed lines from St. John of the Cross: "Return, dove;/For the wounded stag/Looks down from the hill." Lorca stressed the word *wounded*. This wounded stag has of course appeared with various symbolic meanings from the Greeks (Actaeon), through the Middle Ages and down to the time of Ibsen. In the discussion of St. John of the Cross and in his essay in general, Lorca's central emphasis is that poetry springs from anguish, never joy.

In addition to the essays discussed above we need to refer to one other to complete this sketch of Lorca's poetic formation. It is significant that one of his shorter essays, written at a crucial stage in his development (1928), is entitled "Imagination, Inspiration, Evasion." For Lorca, imagination is the talent for discovering the proper metaphorical structure, and inspiration is the poetic gift. But why evasion, a term of negativistic connotation? Lorca suggests that the poet can practice evasion in two ways: by going into irony, where the apparent meaning is really its opposite, or into surrealism, which is "very pure, but not very diaphanous." The poet Luis Cernuda has suggested that both Lorca and Aleixandre employed surrealism as a mask behind which to hide.[5] Lorca, who was torn between rebellion against his Spanish culture and respect for it, in his mature work practiced evasion both through irony and through the mist of surrealism, but this aspect of his work has thus far not been sufficiently studied.

II *The Influence of Tradition:* The Poem of the Cante Jondo (Poema del cante jondo)

During the years 1921–24 Federico García Lorca was attempting to establish himself among many struggling young poets in Madrid, his allegiance inclining now toward the traditional, now toward the new manner. Eventually he produced a great number of poems. In spite of his unwavering dedication to art, however, Lorca was careless with the organization and publication of his books. A selection of these poems called *Songs* (*Canciones*) was not published until 1927, the *Poem of the Cante Jondo* not until 1931. On examining the books we become aware of faulty organization: a group of six "Caprices" ("Caprichos") in *Cante* belongs in *Songs;* in *Songs* a whole group of "Andaluzas," including two of his most famous lyrics, clearly should be in the *Cante.* But the fact that Lorca created two types of poems in the years 1921–24 and remained uncertain as to how to organize them would seem to demonstrate that he was still searching for a permanent manner of expression. In this sub-division of our chapter we shall discuss briefly the *Poem of the Cante Jondo;* in the following, *Songs.*

Lorca's stylization of the traditional Andalusian song in the *Poem of the Cante Jondo*[6] is the culmination of two basic influences. First, in addition to childhood associations (Lorca's father was interested in the *cante*), while still in Granada the musician Manuel de Falla had aroused Lorca's serious interest in folk music generally—not a difficult task, given Lorca's musical talents. In early 1922 Lorca returned to Granada to lecture on the "Primitive Andalusian Cante" and later in the year he and de Falla organized a Festival of the *Cante jondo*. Lorca's essay, which draws heavily on the research of de Falla,[7] attempts to discover the source and the heart of the ancient *cante* in Andalusia. When the gypsies fleeing from Tamerlane's invasions finally reached Spain around 1440 they brought a tradition of song whose elements blended with those already existing to form the *cante,* the oldest form apparently being the gypsy *siguiriya*. This song is characterized by the reiterated use of the same note and a lack of metrical rhythm. Other older forms are the *soleares,* the religious *saetas* and the *peteneras*. Flamenco forms such as the rhythmic *sevillanas* of Seville are of much more recent origin. The literary text of these songs is usually in tercets or quantrains. The themes of the *cante* are the universal ones of love and death, and as Lorca says, "Woman in the *cante jondo* is named Anguish." The purest song for Lorca is one stripped bare by time to its very core, to the essence of Spanish profundity and sadness.

In addition to de Falla's influence on Lorca, there was also that of the poets Salvador Rueda and Manuel Machado, who had reintroduced the Andalusian themes. Machado's *Cante Hondo* (1912), a popularization of the existing Andalusian folk traditions, is actually very close to folk poetry, even to the use of Andalusian localisms. Many of the forms and themes are represented, especially the dialogue of love between man and woman, the anguish of the brevity of love, then hopeless resignation before life itself. But Machado's very success in imitating the folk proved his undoing; García Lorca, who fled folksiness like the plague, correctly surmised that Machado's book would soon be scorned by the poets as common.

Lorca's *Poem of the Cante Jondo* is a brief spiritual geography and history of Andalusia, colored strongly by the poet's own emphases. In a sparse lyric entitled "Poem of the *soleá,*" Lorca defines the total area:

Barren land,
Quiet land,
Land of
Immense nights.

(Tierra seca
tierra quieta
de noches
inmensas.

(Wind in the olive groves,	(Viento en el olivar,
Wind in the mountains.)	viento en la sierra.)
Agéd	Tierra
Land	vieja
Of candle	del candil
And of anguish.	y la pena.)

The area is restricted to that dominated by the great Guadalquivir River, which comes down from the snows to the wheat fields. While the Duero and Genil are rivers without much movement, the Guadalquivir "carries olives, orange blossoms,/Andalusia, to the seas." In a few telling strokes the poet sketches the towns of Seville, Granada, Córdoba, Málaga. For Lorca, "Seville is a tower/Peopled with fine archers . . . /Seville to wound"— and he finds the wounds of Don Juan, the Great Lover of Spanish legend, "bitter." Of Granada, his birthplace, Lorca remembers only the bells of matins and that Granada is "the city that sighs for the sea." Dark and silent Córdoba is the place to die, a theme Lorca developed in his essay on Góngora. His "Malagueña," for the sensual and lively city of Málaga, is surprisingly grim: "Death/enters and departs/from the tavern," a tavern where guitar, smell of salt, sensual presence of the female and "sinister people" come together.

The poet's typical Andalusian setting is a village lost in a place of ancient olive groves, clear water, and with a cross on the bare mountain. The sound of the village is the guitar, "Heart sorewounded/by five swords," the guitarist's fingers. As the poet begins to assert a personal direction, a basic theme which emerges is that of the dead horseman, elaborated in various poems. The poem "Road" begins the theme.

A hundred horsemen in mourning	(Cien jinetes enlutados,
Where will they go? . . .	¿dónde irán? . . .
Not Córdoba nor Seville	Ni a Córdoba ni a Sevilla
Will they see.	llegarán.
Nor Granada, she who sighs	Ni a Granada la que suspira
For the sea.	por el mar.
Those dreaming horses will bear	Esos caballos soñolientos
The riders along	los llevarán,
To the labyrinth of crosses	al laberinto de los cruces
Where trembles the song.	donde tiembla el cantar.)

In a later poem, "The Death of the *Petenera*," "a hundred mares mill around./Their riders are dead." Then in "De Profoundis," "The hundred men in love/forever sleep/Beneath the dry earth" in the ancient city of Córdoba.

In "Surprise," the nameless protagonist has become a single figure tragically alone on the street of the town. Lorca's ability in suggesting in a few lines a feeling of the total isolation of the individual is outstanding. In this bare poem the knife seems only a death symbol, which he was to elaborate later.

Dead he lay in the street	(Muerto se quedó en la calle
With a knife in his breast.	con un puñal en el pecho.
No one knew his name.	No lo conocía nadie.
How the street lamp trembled!	¡ Cómo temblaba el farol!
Mother . . .	Madre.
For dead he lay in the street	Que muerto se quedó en la calle
With a knife in his breast	que con un puñal en el pecho
And no one knew his name.	y que no lo conocía nadie.)

In the section of *saetas*, brief songs which usually show a blend of the lyric and the religious, Lorca introduces some of the religious themes he continued to exploit later. In "Saeta" there is a suggestion of the contrast between the sensuousness of religion in Seville and the asceticism of original Christianity. He describes the Spanish Christ as his figure is carried by in a religious procession:

Dark Christ	(Cristo moreno
Changes from	pasa
The lily of Judea	de lirio de Judea
To red carnation in Spain.	a clavel de España.)

In an example of the *siguiriya* entitled "The Rhythm of the Siguiriya," Lorca has presented the song itself personified as a woman.

Among black butterflies	(Entre mariposas negras,
Goes a dark-skinned lass	va una muchacha morena
Next to a white serpent	junto a una blanca serpiente
Of mist.	de niebla.
Land of light,	Tierra de luz,
Sky of earth.	Cielo de tierra.)

And as he suggested in his discussion of the rhythm of the older *cante*, "The song goes chained to the tremor/of a rhythm that never comes."

Since they are little related to the *Cante jondo*, the group of six "Caprices" which we mentioned earlier should more properly be in *Songs*, but certainly they are ingenious lyrics of multiple suggestion. Typical is "*Crótalo*," the basic part of which follows:

Crótalo.	(Crótalo.
Crótalo.	Crótalo.
Crótalo.	Crótalo.
Sonorous beetle.	Escarabajo sonoro.
In the spider	En la araña
of the hand	de la mano
you ripple	rizas el aire
the torrid air,	cálido,
and drown yourself	y te ahogas en tu trino
in your wooden trill.	de palo.)

The word *crótalo* is here onomatopoeic for the sound of the beetle, but it is also from the Greek word for castanet. In the second stanza, we see that the predominant image becomes that of the castanet in the "spider (perhaps the lines) of the hand," and the image is strengthened by the auditory suggestion. This kind of artistic manipulation of the double image is characteristic of ultraistic poetry.

The *Poem of the Cante Jondo*, even though a partial failure as a unified book, has a central core of lyrics which will endure as some of Lorca's most satisfying work. In the original edition, since apparently the lyrics formed so brief a unit, Lorca included two dramatic sketches of doubtful merit which take up the last third of the book. The first, "Scene of the Lieutenant-Colonel of the Civil Guard," probably proceeding from Valle-Inclán's *The Horns of Don Friolera*, is a sketch of the confrontation of the colonel with a gypsy who seems to have been arrested. The gypsy, with "sulphur and rose on his lips," strangely agitates the colonel, who suddenly falls dead. In the second sketch, a figure called *el Amargo*, "the Embittered One," argues with a Horseman over the disposition of a phallic knife while they lose their way outside Granada. Apparently written around 1925, both pieces involve a deliberate ambiguity shifting between death and homosexual imagery, and in spite of being sources for Lorca's subsequent work, they tend to destroy the harmony of the book. But the profound lyrics remain as an example of Lorca's genius in transmuting popular materials into an artistic form of permanent value.

III *The Influence of Ultraism:* Songs (Canciones)

From the varied collection of poems which he wrote during the formative years 1921–24, Lorca published in 1927 in Madrid an extensive selection entitled *Songs (Canciones),*[8] a book which generally reflects his interest in the practice of ultraism and related vanguard schools. The book shows wide variety, indicating that Lorca was still experimenting, for it includes a section of "Songs for Children," a series of "Three Portraits with Shadow," which have a certain intellectual pretension, and even a section of "Andalusian Pieces" ("Andaluzas"), in the manner of the *Cante jondo.* In the last half of the book, which has puzzled and disturbed critics, Lorca is projecting his turbulent state of mind, and as a group the poems reveal much about the poet but are perraps not first-rate poetry. "Future Life" reveals the poet's struggle with narcissism. A large group of poems falls under the ominous title, "Eros with Walking Cane," in which Lorca projects with irony his sexual attitudes.

Throughout *Songs* there is evidence of Lorca's interest in ultraism, but especially in the section "Theories" he gives us examples of the vanguard manner. Perhaps the strongest example is "Frieze," here quoted complete, with the typographical arrangement of the Spanish exactly as Lorca printed it.

FRIEZE

EARTH	SKY
The lasses of the breeze pass with their long tails.	The lads of the air leap over the moon.

(FRISO

TIERRA	CIELO
Las niñas de la brisa van con sus largas colas.	Los mancebos del aire saltan sobre la luna.)

Here, as the poet intended, we are uncertain whether the lads and lasses are metaphor or reality, and the mind is supposed to remain in suspension.

Although demonstrating some interest in typographical arrangments, Lorca was more impressed by the short poem as a succession of individual scenes, like a series of paintings shown rapidly. Many critics have felt that techniques of the cinema also exerted an influence on poetry at this time. Perhaps his most enduring example is the following:

Three Trees Cut Down	(*Cortaron Tres Arboles*
They were three.	Eran tres.
(Day came with his axes.)	(Vino el día con sus hachas.)
They were two.	Eran dos.
(Trailing wings of silver.)	(Alas rastreras de plata.)
They were one.	Era uno.
They were none.	Era ninguno.
(The water was left bare.)	(Se quedó desnuda el agua.))

The central double image is evoked by the "trailing wings of silver," suggesting the reluctant motion of the shiny axe blades, or the impressive way in which a tree silvered by light seems to trail its branches on falling. Lorca achieved a number of successful lyrics in this manner, most of them depending on image almost entirely.

The section of "Songs for Children" evokes a puzzling and conflicting aspect of Lorca. Some critics have insisted that Lorca was always much like a child, with the assumption that he produced songs of innocence for children. But since we know that Freud's work[9] which armed bitter conflict as to the child's "innocence" was being discussed at this time, we wonder if Lorca's children's poems do not deliberately have other intentions. It seems as if he might have been trying to immerse the guilty "knowing" of adulthood in an "innocent" atmosphere. Lorca's essay "Cradle Songs" may offer some evidence. While Pedrell's famous collection[10] has only songs of the "go to sleep, little one" variety, Lorca unearthed and discusses other types, in one of which the nurse laments her own love-problems to the baby. In *Songs* the little poems are imaginative, but with a hidden meaning the child would certainly miss. For example, even at this time Lorca seems to want to stress the failure of normal marriage relations. In "The Lizard Is Weeping" he charmingly presents Mr. Lizard and Miss Lizard, with her little white apron, both of them weeping. And why? Without wanting to, they have lost their engagement ring, significantly made of lead, not gold. In short, Lorca was apparently trying to say that the period of his songs of innocence had already passed, and indeed hereafter his songs of experience were to bear a certain brand of pain.

The series of "Andalusian Pieces" ("Andaluzas") in *Songs* are actually in Lorca's manner of the *Cante jondo*. Two of these lyrics are perhaps the finest example of Lorca's Andalusian popular poetry. "The Song of the Horseman," for example, appears in almost every anthology containing Lorca's poetry. In this poem the horseman is headed toward dark and silent Córdoba, for Lorca the fitting city in which to face death. But the mysterious and foreboding forces of death threaten the rider even before he reaches the city.

Córdoba.	(Córdoba.
Distant and lonely.	Lejana y sola.
Midnight mare, enormous moon,	Jaca negra, luna grande,
And olives in my saddle pack,	y aceitunas en mi alforja.
Though I know well all the roads,	Aunque sepa los caminos
I'll never get to Córdoba . . .	yo nunca llegaré a Córdoba . . .
Córdoba.	Córdoba.
Distant and lonely.	Lejana y sola.)

Perhaps the most suggestive of the lyrics in the Andalusian manner during this period is "Tree, Olive Tree" ("Arbolé, arbolé"), a ballad-song which evokes popular poetry back to the Middle Ages but at the same time sounds like the *Gypsy Ballads* soon to be written.[11] The text of the poem will facilitate discussion.

[53]

Tree, olive tree,
Dry with green branches.

The lass of fairest countenance
  Is picking olives ripe;
The wind, a gallant of towers high,
  Clasps arms around her waist.
Four horsemen passed before her
    eyes
  On Andalusian mares,
With suits of brightest blue and
    green
And long dark trailing capes.
"Come, lass, come to Granada
    town."
But the girl listens not.
Three bullfighters passed before
    her eyes,
  Slim of waist and bold;
Their suits of lights of color
    orange
  With swords of silver old.
"Come, lass, come to Seville with
    us."
But the girl listens not.
When evening shadows to violet
    turned
  And coming night discloses,
A young man passed who held in
    hand
  Moon-myrtles and red roses.
"Come, lass, come to Granada
    town."
And the girls listens not.
The lass of fairest countenance
  Keeps picking olives ripe,
With the gray arm of the sighing
    wind
  Clinging around her waist.

Tree, olive tree
Dry with green branches.

(Arbolé arbolé
seco y verdé.

  La niña de bello rostro
está cogiendo aceituna.
El viento, galán de torres,
la prende por la cintura.
Pasaron cuatro jinetes,

sobre jacas andaluzas
con trajes de azul y verde,

con largas capas oscuras.
"Vente a Granada, muchacha."

La niña no los escucha.
Pasaron tres torerillos

delgaditos de cintura,
con trajes color naranja

y espada de plata antigua.
"Vente a Sevilla, muchacha."

La niña no los escucha.
Cuando la tarde se puso

morada, con luz difusa,
pasó un joven que llevaba

rosas y mirtos de luna.
"Vente a Granada, muchacha."

Y la niña no lo escucha.
La niña del bello rostro
sigue cogiendo aceituna,
con el brazo gris del viento

ceñido por la cintura.

Arbolé arbolé
seco y verdé.)

The refrain, *"Arbole arbolé,"* which is only the word for *tree* with the accent shifted to an added *é*, is apparently directly from a folk poem, or mostly so. It defies translation, but our English folk song "Tree, Lemon Tree" carries something of the same meaning. The heart of the poem is in the presentation of the wind as a masculine figure, and as a *visual* image. We observe that at the end of the poem the arm of the wind is gray, indicating a loss of vitality. How are we to interpret the symbols? If the girl is the simple feminine, the graying wind suggests a threatened impotence in the masculine (a frequent emphasis in Lorca's poetry). If the girl is the fertile promise of Andalusia, the wind as gallant may well be the masculine spirit always in decline. Lorca insisted that he was part of a "sad and static people;" the effects of the long, agonizing decline of the Arabic and then the Spanish culture in the region caused him continued wonderment.

In the series entitled "Three Portraits with Shadow," each portrait with an accompanying poem, Lorca attempts a structure of some intellectual pretensions. The first portrait, of Verlaine, is obviously not a study of the French poet, but a statement about the work of Lorca, who intones that "The song/I'll never say,/has died on my lips." Apparently Lorca felt at this time that both he and Verlaine wanted to express sexual themes which society had forbidden; probably he was not familiar with the tome of *Secret Poems (Poèmes secrètes)* Verlaine printed privately. In the accompanying poem called "Bacchus" Lorca reveals how the shadow of a fig tree (a sexual symbol) advances threateningly like a panther to dominate his lyric shadow.

The second of the three portraits, "Juan Ramón Jiménez," is not, as some critics have assumed,[12] a praise of the poet, but a subtle criticism. Lorca suggests that Jiménez had so diligently pursued the ineffable in his poetry that he was in danger of losing all human passion. While most critics defend the ineffable in Jiménez, it has for others remained his greatest weakness. The accompanying poem is "Venus," in which Lorca's imagery shifts between the classical and the near biological, not an unusual occurrence among ultraistic poets, most of whom were readers of Freudian literature. The third portrait is "Debussy," a study in narcissism, since the images stress reflections. The final accompanying poem in the series, "Narcissus," portrays Lorca's struggle with the problem of narcissism. Like Jiménez at a certain period, Lorca sought to understand his preoccupation with self, and in extreme moments it is united with thoughts of suicide.

The last half of *Songs* is composed of a group of ironic, enigmatic, troubled and revolutionary sections. Since these poems do not support the legend of Lorca as a popular poet, the critics have tended to ignore them. While admittedly they are not his best poetry, these poems provide some basis for an understanding of the splenetic and rebellious elements in Lorca's later work. In a series of "Caprices" ("Juegos") significantly dedicated to Luis Buñuel, who later became infamous with the scandalous film *The Audalusian Hound,* the most surprising poem is the "Song of the Fairy," a picture of a transvestite adorning himself with a "shameless jasmine." In Spain, custom has generally prohibited the exploitation of abnormal sexuality. The "Eros con bastón" section is an example of Lorca's ingenious irony. Since *bastón* means both "walking cane" and "baton," Lorca must mean either that the love god Eros is limping or that he is fiercely sexual (the baton being an obvious phallic symbol). The poem "Lucy Martínez" expresses normal (although brutal) sensuality: "I come to consume your mouth/and to drag you by the hair." "In Málaga" suggests Lorca's idea of the feminine as crude fertility. In the brief poem "Nu" he tries to comment expansively and ironically on Spanish and French sexual customs. The series "Another World" reveals his self-preoccupation. In "The Crazed Boy" the departing light plays a joke on a boy by separating him from his shadow. This theme is developed further in "Suicide," where the poet struggles with self-absorption. The section promisingly entitled "Love" is disappointing, since the narcissistic theme is continued, and the vague poems which follow explore a passion which will not quite tell its name.

The section called "Songs to Conclude" contains one forceful lyric in which the poet projects his turbulent and confused direction for the future.

The bonfire thrusts into the fields of afternoon	(La higuera pone al campo de la tarde
Antlers of an infuriated stag . . .	unas astas de ciervo enfurecido . . .

The essential things are upon me.	Llegan mis cosas esenciales.
They are refrains of refrains.	Son estribillos de estribillos.
Among the reeds and late afternoon,	Entre los juncos y la baja tarde,
How strange that Federico should be my name!	¡qué raro que me llame Federico!)

In the first line the fused image of fire, stag and raging antlers suggests turbulent passion; the last line reflects the poet's struggle to retain his identity.

When *Songs* appeared in 1927, the critics were puzzled and still vaguely disappointed in Lorca. The poet Gerardo Diego, then still defending poetry as intellectual play, perhaps came closest to penetrating the poems. Diego in a review of the book commented on Lorca's manner of forcing together the innocent and the perverse, and felt that the poems simply failed to show unity. Diego chastised Lorca for excessive frivolity, concluding a bit smugly: "It is fine to play at writing poetry, but not too much." [13] Surely Lorca, whose evasion was cloaking serious problems of identity and adjustment, must have felt himself even more isolated from his Spanish heritage.

CHAPTER 3

Gypsy Ballads (Romancero gitano)

WHEN we pass from the earlier books of poetry of García Lorca and begin the *Gypsy Ballads* (*Romancero gitano*), very soon we become conscious of the fact that there is a quickening, an urgency, a power that builds almost without slackening throughout the book. And even on second or third reading the same reaction occurs. This reaction does not depend upon what has been called the mystery in the poems, for much of the mystery can be traced to an ignorance of Lorca's symbols and of his thematic purposes. Much of the emotion generated in the ballads is intensely personal and private. But there is a proper relation among form, metaphorical structure and personal thematic purpose, so that we can remain suspended among these elements in an atmosphere of poetry. It is of importance to observe that, while almost all eighteen ballads have narrative and dramatic elements, Lorca was struggling to focus the poetic impact to drive home his personal lyric theme. Perhaps the best way to conceive the effect of the book is to imagine it as a painting, in which Lorca's dark, brooding face is centrally predominant, surrounded by the characters and scenes depicted in the individual ballads.

The theme of the *Gypsy Ballads* must be expressed with care. Lorca himself discounted the thematic importance of the gypsy by insisting that the book "is gypsy only in some parts [*algún trozo*] at the beginning." He went on to say generally: "In its essence it is an Andalusian tableau [*retablo andaluz*]." Then he narrows his idea to conclude that the ballads actually "have a single essential protagonist: Granada."—that is, we suggest, ultimately Lorca himself. For Lorca saw his native Granada in a very personal way: "Granada is the persecuted, which, instead of protesting, turns into a dance . . ."[1]

Now if the book is to reveal the Andalusian temperament, as

Lorca said, we may suspect that it will involve sensuality and religious fervor. And indeed, the predominant specific theme of the *Gypsy Ballads* is the omnipresence of the sexual instincts, not love but mere physical passion, passion normal and prohibited, passion repressed and incestuous. Lorca was aware that in presenting certain sexual themes he was entering forbidden territory, for he later promised Guillén never to touch the subject again.[2] Also important is the religious theme, which appears in at least four ballads, but, as we shall see, Lorca presents this theme highly colored by his personal attitudes. And since this sexual and religious passion often involves suppression and repression, it easily develops into aggression, and aggression into death.[3] Obviously this pattern of passion to repression to death follows the emphases of psychology in the 1920's, and we believe it is proper to discuss the *Gypsy Ballads* generally from this standpoint.

Lorca's use of the gypsy world to express his own concerns invokes the importance of myth in his work. At this time the work of Freud, Jung, Rank and others which stressed the importance of myth and archetypal symbol was popular, but we do not know how well Lorca understood their work. At least the critic Gustavo Correa has interpreted much of Lorca's work, and especially the *Gypsy Ballads*, as being in the tradition of myth.[4] In choosing primitive gypsy life Lorca could utilize in natural setting elements of nature (moon, star) and animals (horse, bull) with some suggestion of cosmic meaning. Perhaps it is correct to say that Lorca utilized the gypsy traditions to create a kind of personal mythology.

Certainly Lorca's personal view of the world prohibits our always understanding his gypsies by comparing them with the historical gypsy. Since Lorca soon became irritated with his reputation as a "gypsy" poet, obviously he had no lasting interest in the gypsies for themselves. If we focus on the enduring qualities of the gypsy within his group, we can best see him as a specimen of simple, proud, and unyielding manhood; we see the gypsy woman as a passionate figure eager to assume the respected position of a wife. Now it is significant that in the *Gypsy Ballads* Lorca has chosen to focus on other than these noble qualities. A partial explanation of his attitude can be traced to the fact that the Andalusian gypsy has become changed from the historical type.[5] In

Spain the government by an earlier decree tried to force the gypsies to settle permanently in the cities; typically, they have of course been nomads. Lorca thought the gypsies lived under a matriarchy in Spain; historically their groups have been generally patriarchal.[6] The fact that Lorca presented his gypsies as unbridled instinct indicates that he was employing them predominantly to emphasize his chosen theme.

As the title *Gypsy Ballads* indicates, García Lorca after earlier experimentation finally settled on the form of the Spanish ballad (*romance*), a tradition kept alive by important poets since the 16th century. In the Golden Age Lope de Vega and Góngora, among many others, were important in creating a neo-artistic ballad, which incorporated lyric elements while retaining narrative content. This tradition was continued by José Zorrilla in the Romantic period and finally passed to the Machados and Juan Ramón Jiménez in the early 20th century. Jiménez, who had published earlier a book entitled *Pastorals* (*Pastorales*) in ballad form, in 1924 wrote and sent to Lorca's sister a ballad called "Generalife," which suggests unmistakably the ring of the *Gypsy Ballads*.[7] Lorca, as had Jiménez before him, struggled to avoid creating mere popular ballads of local color, a type which merited only scorn among their fellow poets.

While in form Lorca's ballads are quite traditional, what distinguishes the style and provides the basis for the "Lorquian manner" is the metaphor. It is partly like that of Góngora, but rarely depends on displacement of syntax or classical reference. The Lorquian form is somewhat like the ultraistic manner, but is worked into the narrative flow. Lorca's images often depend upon the displacement of the elements of the action itself. Two critical books devoted entirely to Lorca's metaphorical technique indicate the complexity of his poetic style.[8] We shall discuss pertinent examples in the analysis of individual ballads.

The first of the poems, the "Ballad of the Moon," plunges us at once into the mysterious and difficult imagery and metaphor of the *Gypsy Ballads*. The opening lines introduce the characters and setting:

The moon descended to the forge	(La luna vino a la fragua
In her bustled skirt of white.	con su polisón de nardos.

Gypsy Ballads

The boy-child looks and looks at her,	El niño la mira, mira.
The child stares at the sight	El niño la está mirando.)

The forge as setting suggests the magic world of the gypsies as workers of fine metals, a tradition which goes back to alchemy and supernatural creation with metals.[9] The moon as white (not typical of Lorca) suggests the feminine, and since the bustle was associated in his mind with the previous generation, surely the moon is here a mother figure. In the significant lines which follow, the "moon shows, lascivious and pure, her breasts of hard tin." This imagery of adjectival contrasts is continued when the moon figure tells the boy the gypsies will find him "on the anvil with his little eyes closed." While the anvil is natural in this setting, it is significant that Lorca in "Ballad of the Dark Anguish" used anvil to mean "breast." The boy is fascinated, but urges the moon figure to flee, for the gypsies of "bronze and dream" will make her into trinkets. But at the end, "Through the heavens the moon is ascending/With a child held by the hand," while back at the forge the gypsies are raising cries of mourning in a watchful air.

While this ballad defies conclusive analysis, it seems to us Lorca has blended gypsy mythology of moon and metalworking with Freudian psychology. Surely the "lascivious" attraction of the boy to the feminine or mother figure, whom he must reject because to him she is "pure," is the significant direction. Indeed, the ballad is a stylized dance of attraction and rejection. Perhaps Lorca has exerted a personal emphasis in that the boy ultimately departs with the moon figure. While Spanish critics have generally concluded that the scene depicts the death of the boy, we argue simply that the gypsies are lamenting the boy's not-normal separation from the group. This ballad is a fine blending of the innocent tinged with a suggestion of the attraction of the flesh; even after many readings the action and suggestion remain suspended among multiple meanings not capable of adequate summary.

In three of the ballads the central figure is a woman, and in each case she is reacting to the presence of the sexual. In "Preciosa and the Air," Lorca with exaggerated imagery attempts to elevate the simple action to an unreal plane from the beginning:

Beating upon a parchment moon	(Su luna de pergamino
Preciosa starts to pass	Preciosa tocando viene
Along a dark amphibious trail	por un anfibio sendero
Of laurel and crystal glass.	de cristales y laureles.)

The "amphibious" becomes clear when it is followed by "night filled with fishes," since the fish is a standard sexual symbol in Lorca. Preciosa is near the towers where the English live (toward Gibraltar perhaps); the English are a convenient example of unruffled and passionless ordinariness.

Preciosa has not gone far when she is accosted by big St. Christopher, whose words of oriental-tinged imagery come as a shock, even though the color blue is here innocence: "Lass, let me lift up your skirts,/Let me examine you,/And open with my ancient fingers/Your belly's rose of blue." Her action is swift: "Preciosa casts aside the drum/And flees without a word;/The wind-giant stalks behind the girl/Wielding a flaming sword." Lorca was proud of his creation of this myth of anthropomorphic wind; actually of course there is a classic predecessor in Ovid and in Lorca's own poem "*Arbolé arbolé.*" Preciosa escapes by taking refuge in the house of the English consul, who calmly offers her warm milk to drink while the furious wind tears at the rooftop outside. The theme of the ballad is therefore the great shock of innocence confronted by frightening pansexuality.

As for "The Gypsy Nun," its mood is sustained quietness, although we are warned initially that there are "Thistles in the fine grasses." After a somewhat forced image of the church that "growls in the distance/like a bear belly upward," Lorca presents a delicate psychological revelation as the nun embroiders her erotic stirrings into the cloth, the "flowers of her fantasy." Significantly they are big, bold flowers, the sunflower and the magnolia, in bright colors. Then her attention is distracted:

Within the eyes of the nun	(Por los ojos de la monja
Gallop two horsemen bold;	galopan dos caballistas.
A tremor muffled and remote	Un rumor último y sordo
Disturbs her garment's folds.	le despega la camisa.)

But the nun goes back to embroidering the erotic disturbance into the flowers on the cloth. This ballad exemplifies how important it was for Lorca to keep a delicate suspension of theme, for here he is dangerously close to the naturalistic (and some would say the Freudian) conclusion that everyone has low passions.

One of the outstanding ballads is the "Ballad of the Dark Anguish," which begins with a typical Lorquian image of fused action and situation: "The beaks of the eager cockerels/Dig, seeking out the dawn." Soledad Montoya of the poem is not only the personification of the "woman named Anguish," as Lorca saw her in the *Cante jondo;* she is also strangely almost a double of Lorca himself. One thing she is not, however; the terrifying figure who comes storming down out of the mountains is no real woman:

Her flesh of yellowed copper smells	(Cobre amarillo, su carne,
Of shadow and stallion strong;	huele a caballo y a sombra.
The smoke-hued anvils of her breasts	Yunques ahumados sus pechos,
Are moaning rounded songs.	gimen canciones redondas.)

Soledad, who comes seeking "her joy and her person," suffers a dark anguish whose cause is the bitter passion dammed up in her, a passion specifically erotic: "Ay, my gowns of linen fine/My thighs of poppy red!"

Although the poem begins in the dark and goes toward the light, Soledad, who is bronzed at the beginning, seems under the pressure of her passion to become dun and even black as jet. But the poet, who has been in dialogue with her, tells her to "bathe her body with water of morning larks," that is, to transmute her pain into song. In the short conclusion to the poem, Lorca brings together Soledad, the gypsies and the poet into a company beset by permanent anguish, with little hope for the future.

O anguish of the gypsy race!	(¡O pena de los gitanos!
Clear anguish always alone.	Pena limpia y siempre sola.
O anguish of a hidden source	¡O pena de cauce oculto
And such a distant dawn!	y madrugada remota!)

Then there is the ballad which has become the most quoted, memorized, recited and maligned, that of "The Unfaithful Wife."

It is a masterpiece of normal sensuality; therefore the public has responded to the flashy but easily grasped imagery. Indeed much of Lorca's popular reputation can be traced to the fact that this ballad has been incorrectly read as characteristic of Lorca and of the whole volume of *Gypsy Ballads*.

With the laconic prolongation of an octosyllable ("Well, then, I took her down by the river") the gypsy protagonist sets the scene for an episode as old as man. Lorca, in a statement perhaps only poetically correct rather than literally true, declared that he once heard a gypsy say this line. The gypsy thought the girl was a maiden but in reality she had a husband, a point critics have made much of; actually the girl's response certainly betokens experience. The Lorquian imagery describing the setting is very fine; the images of flowering sexuality are overpowering. The gypsy sums up the episode in purely popular fashion: "That night I travelled the best of all roads,/mounted on a pearly mare/without bridle or stirrups." The picture of the girl after the event has a fine sensitivity: "Soiled with kisses and with sand/she was taken back from the river." Lorca has the gypsy say, "I acted the way I am,/Like a true gypsy," and these words are correct, whether Lorca was aware of it or not, for all the other gypsies in the book show the effects of his personal attitudes for thematic purposes.

As another example of overwhelming passion between the sexes, Lorca returned to the popular Biblical theme of the incestuous love of Amnon for Thamar. In the Golden Age Tirso de Molina had written a turgid drama on this theme which Lorca must have known. But whereas Tirso in his play concentrates on motives and suggests condemnation of the act, Lorca focusses insistently on the rabid Amnon before and during the seduction itself. With the moon wheeling in the sky over an earth without waters, Thamar is singing nude on the terrace, and the imagery conveys frigidity. Amnon, however, "his loins brimming with spume," writhes in desire as he contemplates in the moon "the steely breasts of his sister." The poet sustains this tension at length, the natural surroundings becoming embroiled: "Ivy of feverish chills/Covers his burning flesh." Finally the brutal seduction occurs, and in the aftermath the imagery becomes so shocking that Spanish critics have usually treated it with silence. As Luis Cernuda has suggested, the dramatic tone of the *Gypsy Ballads* is often at the point of becoming too theatrical to be convincing.[10] While the poet's method is wearing a bit thin in this the last ballad in the book (as Lorca arranged them originally), it still succeeds in presenting a world cosmically awry.

While in the ballads previously discussed the imagery is sometimes shocking, it was when Lorca began to project male characters that his intentions most nearly approached the prohibited in traditional Spain. Therefore he used his poetic skills of evasion by creating mystery so effectively that his meaning has remained obscure for many readers. Critics have tended to emphasize the mysterious in the ballads, especially where psychological penetration such as Schonberg's seemed to attack the traditional picture of Lorca. But the ballads that still remain to be considered here must be faced honestly and frankly if we are to understand Lorca's purpose. Of all the ballads, his favorite was the "Somnambulistic Ballad," and since his fellow poets testify to his power in reciting the poem and to its effect on him, surely its meaning is to some degree a part of his personal and artistic self.[11] Since our inclusion of quotations has had to be limited, perhaps it will be instructive in suggesting the impact of imagery, sound and narrative technique to offer at more length a significant portion of this important ballad.

Green is the color, bewitching green,	(Verde que te quiero verde.
Green winds, green-tinted fountain;	Verde viento. Verdes ramas.
Boat upon a far off sea,	El barco sobre la mar
Stallion on the mountain.	y el caballo en la montaña.
With shadow on her waist she waits	Con la sombra en la cintura
Behind her railing dreaming,	ella sueña en su baranda,
Greenish flesh, hair of green,	verde carne, pelo verde,
Her eyes cold silver gleaming.	con ojos de fría plata.
Green is the color, bewitching green . . .	Verde que te quiero verde . . .
The fig tree scrubs against the wind	La higuera frota su viento
The abrasion of its wands,	con la lija de sus ramas,
And the mountain, skulking catamount,	y el monte, gato garduño,
His bitter hackles stands.	eriza sus pitas agrias.

But who approaches? And from
    whence?
Behind her railing she—
Greenish flesh, hair of green—
    Dreams of the bitter sea.
"Comrade, how I'd like to change
    My stallion for a home,
My saddle for a mirror bright,
    My sheath-knife for a comb;
Friend, from the mountain pass
    at Cabra
    All wet with blood I come."
"If I but could, my lad, we would
    At once agreement find,
But I no longer am myself
    My house no longer mine." . . .
"Let me climb once more at least
    Up to the lofty railing,
I must, I must once more ascend
    Up to the greenish railing,
Verandah of the moon from where
    The waters are ever falling.

Now the two companions climb
    Up to the lofty railing,
Leaving behind a trail of blood,
    The tears behind them trail-
      ing. . . .
"Companion, tell me, where is
    she?
    Where has your grieved lass
    gone?
How many times she waited for
    you,
    How many would wait again,
Blooming face and raven hair,
    Behind this railing green!"

Upon the countenance of the
    cistern
    The gypsy girl was floating,
Greenish flesh, hair of green,
    Her eyes cold silver frozen.

¿Pero quién vendrá? ¿Y por
    dónde . . . ?
Ella sigue en su baranda,
verde carne, pelo verde,
soñando en la mar amarga.
Compadre, quiero cambiar
mi caballo por su casa,
mi montura por su espejo,
mi cuchillo por su manta.
Compadre, vengo sangrando,

desde los puertos de Cabra.
Si yo pudiera, mocito,
ese trato se cerraba.
Pero yo ya no soy yo,
ni mi casa es ya mi casa. . . .
Dejadme subir al menos
hasta las altas barandas,
¡dejadme subir!, dejadme
hasta las altas barandas,
Barandales de la luna
por donde retumba el agua.

Ya suben los dos compadres
hasta las altas barandas,
Dejando un rastro de sangre.
Dejando un rastro de
    lágrimas. . . .
¡Compadre! ¿Dónde está, dime?

¿Dónde está tu niña amarga?

¡Cuántas veces te esperó!

¡Cuántas veces te esperara,
cara fresca, negro pelo,
en esta verde baranda!

Sobre el rostro del aljibe

se mecía la gitana.
Verde carne, pelo verde,
con ojos de fría plata.

Gypsy Ballads

An icicle from the moon sustains
   Her upon the water there.
Then night became as intimate
   As a tiny village square.
Drunken Civil Guards began
   To beat upon the door.
Green is the color, bewitching
     green,
   Green winds, green-tinted
     fountain,
Boat upon a far off sea,
   Stallion on the mountain.

Un carámbano de luna
la sostiene sobre el agua.
La noche se puso íntima
como una pequeña plaza.
Guardias civiles borrachos
en la puerta golpeaban.
Verde que te quiero verde.

Verde viento. Verdes ramas.

El barco sobre la mar.
Y el caballo en la montaña.)

The refrain or leitmotif in the first line (which is literally "Green, how much I want you, green") is, as Jiménez has pointed out, from a line of a folk song which goes on, "like the color of olives"—that is, the dark olive complexion of Andalusia. Lorca's imaginative leap in fixing upon the green began with a specific point of reference. Actually the phrase refers to Dalí, at the time very close to Lorca. According to Dalí's sister, Dalí, although very handsome, had a "greenish" cast to his complexion, supposedly because of Moorish blood. Green is associated usually with the specifically erotic in Lorca. There is little doubt that Dalí understood the personal suggestion in the poem. It is interesting to see how he, much less sensual than Lorca, many years later rejects the implications of the leitmotif in a novel by expressing the opposite attitude toward the color: "Green, how I detest you, green." [12]

From the standpoint of Lorca's purpose, then, the "Somnambulistic Ballad" is a phantasy of homosexual attraction, with the problems of the feminine and of identity intermixing in the shadowy narration. From the beginning "She," half feminine, half death, is present, but already her unseeing eyes of "frozen silver" indicate her frozen power. Then the two comrades appear, both struggling for identity. The two climb up to the high balcony and disappear toward the moon itself, from where the sexual waters are streaming. One of the comrades recalls how a real lass used to wait for him on the "green verandah," but when the scene shifts a gypsy girl, now dead, is floating on the cistern. Finally, for just the briefest of instants, there occurs almost the only moment of rest in the agitated world of the *Gypsy Ballads*, when "night became intimate." But this peace is shattered by the Civil Guard, here representing reality and social restriction. Then the poet returns to his leitmotif of green.

In passing, the interplay between night and day in this and other ballads needs some comment for the English reader. Lorca adapted his night-day structure from St. John of the Cross (with of course no mystic intent on Lorca's part); St. John achieved his mystic union with God in a "dark night," separated utterly from the world. Lorca in a sonnet evokes his "night of the soul for always dark." [13] In the "Somnambulistic Ballad" the brief moment of tranquility comes at darkest night, just before the dawn. Lorca's specific use of night-day, with a sense of evasion, therefore seems like a perversion of St. John of the Cross, but in the broadest sense we can say that for Lorca night was the time which released the senses and the imagination, while day brought back reality and restriction.

The "Somnambulistic Ballad" illustrates perhaps better than any other Lorca's genius for sustaining various levels of meaning, from the intensely personal to cosmic suggestion, with touches of the primitive, the psychological and the vanguard artistic. Admittedly many readers, not having read the ballad as we have, have been content with its sound and mystery. It is instructive to compare this ballad with A. E. Housman's "Hell's Gate," both as to theme and form. Certainly a close comparison of these two ballads will cast light on the mysterious and perplexing world of both poets.

Although Lorca cloaks it under historical guise, the "Burlesque History of Don Pedro, Knight" is a full-blown example of the surrealist-Freudian manner.[14] Properly it is a kind of travesty of Lope de Vega's drama, *The Horseman of Olmedo;* it is also vaguely reminiscent of the irony of Antonio Machado's "Don Guido." Although Spanish critics have in general said little about the poem, Díaz-Plaja in a brief, evasive phrase identified it correctly as being "like a canvas of Giorgio de Chirico." [15] Chirico with his representations of Freudian dream images was a prime influence on Salvador Dalí, and through him an influence on Lorca.

In the ballad, Don Pedro, weeping darkly, sets out on the journey of life, riding a horse without bridle, symbolic of an unbridled sexual force. The narrative passages are stopped with pauses, after each of which a recurring scene of waters appears. These waters seem to be sexual, narcissistic and probably suicidal; certainly they are ominous. Don Pedro arrives at a religious city, a symbol of the Catholic city, and the people come out to meet him. But Don Pedro, undecided, departs from the city. His people search for him, but find only his "somber horse," dead, a suggestion of impotence. This suggestion is repeated in a striking image: "Unicorn of absence breaks/Into crystal shards his horn." In the final scene, Don Pedro seems to be under the waters: "Over the frozen flower/Is Don Pedro, forgotten,/Ay, playing with the frogs!" And what is the "burla," the burlesque in the ballad? Don Pedro, who set out on a noble but difficult quest, has come down to this final scene, which in context deliberately suggests a masturbation phantasy.[16]

If the *Gypsy Ballads* were to portray Andalusia, as Lorca insisted, it was inevitable that along with the expression of sexual instincts there should be some representation of religious influence, since these powerful forces have remained in tension there, as indeed in all of Spain. In this area García Lorca was of course only following a tradition important to the Generation of 1898, who expressed persistently their hostility to the religious teaching they had received. Arturo Barea in *Lorca the Poet and His People* has developed the background of religious and sexual attitudes in Andalusia. Barea finds an outstanding example in Gabriel Miró's novel, *The Leprous Bishop*. When a schoolboy is found studying pictures of women saints, the religious Father as punishment has him peruse the terrible pictures of martyred saints, drawn and quartered, bloody. These forbidden pictures came to exert a troubling fascination for the boy.[17]

In some of the *Gypsy Ballads*, especially "Martyrdom of St. Eulalia" and "St. Michael," "St. Gabriel" and "St. Raphael," Lorca is writing in this tradition of religious emphasis, and for the moment has dropped the presentation of gypsy characters. The least difficult of the poems is the "Martyrdom of St. Eulalia," but the sustained effect of the gory details is almost overwhelming. Drawing on traditional sources such as the books of saints, Lorca makes historical details seem crudely present. After an ominous scene of Mérida, he concentrates on Eulalia's torture, especially in this part: "The Consul asks for a tray/for the breasts of Olalla. Her sex trembles like a bird/caught in the brambles." In the holes where her breasts were, rivulets of white milk trickle. The Consul carries away her "smoked breasts" on a tray. Eulalia is then hanged on a tree. Finally, angels and seraphim cry, "Holy, holy, holy." Surely this is enough to confirm Lorca's intention to suggest that the subjection of an adolescent's sensitive mind to this kind of material left him with permanent images floating painfully between the erotic and the saintly. Lorca retained this image of the detached breasts, apparently with a confusion of mother, lover, madonna never quite clarified.

The three ballads for the great saints, "St. Michael," "St. Raphael," and "St. Gabriel," subtitled respectively "Granada," "Córdoba," "Sevilla," continue to reveal primarily religious and psychological emphasis, with a criticism of the religious structure approaching viciousness, although critics have tended to evoke a historical tour of the cities to begin their discussions of them. These ballads of difficult interpretation are saturated with Lorca's special ideas and personal symbolism. The ballad "St. Michael," as Lorca initially conceived it, concerns a pilgrimage; therefore we have some base for interpreting the initial scene. As in the "Somnambulistic Ballad," there is an interplay between the desired night and the "brackish dawn," when the waters (of vitality, etc.) become cold and untouchable. Within this scene the important symbols are the mules and the sunflowers. Although it is easy to be too clever in interpreting Lorca, we are inclined to think that the mules in this embroiled scene represent repression and stifling guilt; the sunflowers are the young men on the pilgrimage, who are missing in the scene which follows. (The word for sunflower may also mean "sycophant" in Spanish.)

The scene then shifts to St. Michael in the tower of the church. Here Lorca's intention is clear. St. Michael, who was the paladin, the anchor, the mighty defender of the faith usually depicted with a sword, now is "domesticated," his beautiful thighs covered with lace, pretending a "sweet wrath." Barea has insisted that these details regarding the popular feminization of St. Michael in Andalusia are correct. The Saint is "Fragrant with water of Cologne/ And distant from the flowers," that is, the waters of life have become artificial, and he no longer bears importantly on it.

As the scene shifts to the cathedral, the poet presents a sad Mass attended by "upright gentlemen" and "ladies of doleful mien"—the young men are conspicuously absent. The young women are presented with crude focus on the physical aspects of fertility:

The wenches gather for the Mass
  Eating sunflower seeds,
Their bottoms big and mysterious
  Like planets copper-hued.
	(Vienen manolas comiendo
	semillas de girasoles,
	los culos grandes y ocultos
	como planetas de cobre.)

Even the phrase "eating sunflower seeds" probably has a double meaning. Here at Mass it obviously suggests casualness and commonness, and connected with the first scene of the poem it implies Lorca's insistent idea of the feminine as devourer of the masculine. But the Bishop is an alien figure as he says Mass for the two lines of people, one for women, one for men. The final scene returns to St. Michael, quiet and ineffective in his tower.

The ballad "St. Raphael" for Córdoba is perhaps the most difficult of all to interpret, for in it Lorca not only was being deliberately evasive because of the subject but he has also projected an interplay between a series of dualities all somewhat interrelated. The usual criticism has not even approached Lorca's purpose. In the first part, the "closed coaches" are a difficult symbol, rarely used by Lorca; probably the closed coaches, generally a womb symbol, mean in this ballad that the feminine is absent in the struggle which follows. At this point the initial duality is set up, for we see things double, once in reality, once reflected in the river. Gradually Córdoba becomes two, a "Córdoba of reeds" and a "Córdoba of architecture." At one level the reeds suggest the Arabic in Córdoba, the architecture the Roman, since the great piece of architecture, the Bridge over the Guadalquivir, is Roman. But the gradual emphasis toward the bridge that "blows ten murmurings of Neptune" invokes a suggestion of the bridge as homosexual. Córdoba, an ancient city, an interplay between shadow and architecture "no longer trembles at this confusing mystery." At the private level, the reeds-architecture symbols had special meaning, the reeds (as phallic) suggesting vitality and Lorca; the architecture, artistic creation and Dalí. Indeed, some of

Dalí's paintings after 1927, such as "Font" and "Nostalgic Echo," provide meaningful commentary on this poem.

The second part at its most meaningful level projects a group of boys (*niños*) at that moment of Oedipal struggle when they are suspended between manhood and regression. As the section begins, "A single fish in the water/joins the two Córdobas together." Now this fish symbol, at its broadest spectrum, is not only sexuality (usual in Lorca) but also Christianity, and the continuation corroborates this meaning. Central to the section are "The young lads of impassive face" who are disrobing by the river, lads who are "apprentices of Tobias." Here we must sketch Tobias' story (as it appears in the Spanish encyclopedia). Tobias went out on an important journey, accompanied by the angel Raphael. As they came down to a river, a great fish threatened them, but they killed the fish and saved gall from it to anoint the eyes of Tobias' father, who was blind. Raphael and Tobias returned, were successful in restoring the father's eyesight, and Tobias married and became normally prosperous. Thus Tobias with Raphael's help is successful in what Freud termed the Oedipal struggle. In Lorca's ballad, the young lads are at the point of decision, suspended between "flowers of wine" and "half-moon leaps," the latter probably the homosexual image. The part of Raphael is extremely significant in Lorca's poem, for, no longer protector and defender, he has become "Moorish" and is himself seeking "murmur and cradle," certainly unable to help the lads achieve normal manhood. There are of course other related symbolic suggestions in the ballad, most of them too obscure and personal for convincing interpretation. The poet at the end leaves Córdoba a duality, a Córdoba whose waters are reduced to the spurts of a fountain, and a Córdoba celestial but barren.

The ballad "St. Gabriel" (subtitled "Sevilla") reveals Lorca's usual interplay between the innocent-primitive and the knowing-psychological. The ballad's setting in Seville is the traditional home of Don Juan and hence the city of romance. It is also the Seville of the intense Holy Week. As Spanish critics have pointed out, the Andalusian tends to treat religious figures and ideas with great familiarity, to relate them easily to his own life. Still, Lorca's treatment of the Annunciation as re-expressed in terms of a gypsy girl is not only imaginative but daring. Usually the romantic exchange between the sexes is obligatory in Seville, but Lorca first presents his Don Juan in sad isolation, his usual reluctant bridegroom.

A beautiful lad straight as a reed,	(Un bello niño de junco,
Slim waist and shoulders wide,	anchos hombros, fino talle,
Skin like nocturnal apple dark,	piel de nocturna manzana,
Sad mouth and enormous eyes,	boca triste y ojos grandes,
With nerve of silver like a flame	nervio de plata caliente
He prowls the deserted street.	ronda la desierta calle.)

This pretty lad is all too typical of the effeminate type of masculine figure in the *Gypsy Ballads*. In spite of rather desperate efforts by the critics to convince us otherwise, Lorca was generally unable or unwilling to conceive of mature manhood. In an ingenious Jungian image apparently the act of fertilization takes place in a mythic manner: "His shoes of patent leather break/The dahlias of the air/In double cadence . . ." But Lorca's choice of the dahlia, a scentless and sterile-like flower, casts doubt on the fertilization.

In the second part of the ballad the gypsy girl Anunciación de los Reyes, whose magnificent name indicates the Spanish sense of individuality and worth, has a dramatic encounter, imagined vividly enough to seem real, with the angel Gabriel. To Lorca, Gabriel is only a "Tamer of little doves," but to the girl he is as important as life itself. The angel reveals to her that she is with child, and she accepts the fact with joy. Of course Anunciación is all motherhood, she is the "Mother of a hundred dynasties." Lorca predisposes the unborn infant to the curse of passion and aggression, for in his little voice already there "tremble three bullets of green almond." In general, the ballad is another of Lorca's many problem poems. While it evokes a feeling of tenderness, his intention was apparently to suggest a confusion around the idea of the Virgin Birth, from the beginning a problem for the Church.

Thus far we have been discussing ballads of an outpouring of sexual vitality which often cannot find a proper channel, and in at least three ballads this energy is turned to open aggression. The ballad "Fracas" (originally entitled "Fracas among Young Men") on the surface is a description of a knife fight in which a young gypsy is killed. But from the first lines Lorca complicates the imagery with sexual overtones, mixing the sexual, the aggressive and even the angelic in a brilliant manner which suggests a painting. The knives of Albacete, vaguely phallic, "gleam like fishes." After the gypsy boy falls dead, black angels with great wings like these knives of Albacete come to comfort him. When the judge comes to review the case, he tells the Civil Guard pontifically: "Here we have the same old story, four Romans dead, five Carthaginians." And as the group moves away Lorca persists in focusing the concentrated light of the afternoon into a powerful erotic image:

The afternoon gone mad with fig trees,	(La tarde loca de higueras
While fiery murmurs play,	y de rumores calientes
Falls fainting on their wounded thighs	cae desmayada en los muslos
As the horsemen move away.	heridos de los jinetes.)

Then there are the two ballads on the arrest and death of Antoñito el Camborio. Surely there are few poems in Lorca which invoke more strongly in the reader the mixed emotions of admiration, sympathy and irritation. Antoñito is presented in the "Arrest of Antoñito el Camborio" as a pretty lad, with carefully curled locks, walking along mincingly to see the bullfights in Seville. He also feels that his male cousins envy him his "smooth complexion of olive and jasmine." Along he comes with a willow cane in his hand, the cane obviously phallic, and stops to throw in the water lemons, which are also sexual symbols. At this point Lorca projects ambiguity, for under an elm Antoñito meets a Civil Guard, who leads him off "arm in arm." Since Antoñito is arrested later by five Guards, the meaning is left confused. But a key phrase typifies Antoñito, "moreno de verde luna," a dark man, under the sign of the green moon. This dark one, lonely and persecuted, is in the final anlysis the homosexual type in Lorca's work.

The ballad of the "Death of Antoñito el Camborio" which follows is in some ways one of the most intense of the *Gypsy Ballads*, being marred only by the reason for Antoñito's death. Lorca makes it clear that Antoñito was killed by his cousins because he lacked manhood; he was not that ancient gypsy who stood manly and tall. But, although Antoñito preferred preening to fighting, when the cousins goad him into action he gives a good account of himself. In form and image, the ballad is exceptional from the opening lines: "Voices of death were ringing out/Along the Guadalquivir." The ballad is written in a rare assonance in the high vowel "i," which perhaps suggests high-pitched urgency near a scream. There are some fine images of things being awry: the "stars were thrusting lances/into the gray waters," "the young fighting bulls were dreaming flame-tinted verónicas." But the four cousins are overwhelming odds, and Antoñito falls in a pool of blood, calling on a brother: "Ay, Federico García,/call out for the Civil Guards." Lorca therefore put his personal stamp on this powerful ballad.

But it is perhaps in the "Ballad of the Spanish Civil Guard" that Lorca offers his finest projection of aggression and persecution. In the ballad, it is interesting to see how Lorca subtly reverses the usual roles of the Civil Guard and the gypsy, since normally the Guard would represent order, the gypsies a disrupting social force. From the beginning the poet sustains a high tension as the Guards ominously approach the peaceful gypsy village. The ballad begins as a chromatic study in black:

Black as shadows are the horses, (Los caballos negros son.
  The horseshoes also black; Las herraduras son negras.
Upon the riders' gleaming capes Sobre las capas relucen
  Are stains of ink and wax. manchas de tinta y de cera.

Out of the night they come, their "souls of patent leather," and suggesting "a vague astronomy of shadow pistols"; these are aggression symbols.

Meanwhile, the gypsy village floats between reality and dream, the gypsies going about their business of creating at the forges. Apparently there is a kind of religious celebration going on, with figures of Joseph and the Virgin dressed in the traditional fashion of Andalusia. The scene shifts to the Guard, advancing with an air of doom: "A murmur of immortelles (graveyard flowers)/Invades their cartridge belts." The scene shifts rapidly to the gypsies again, all innocence and sociability: "The city free from fear/Multiplied her doors." Then in a tumultuous scene the Guard swoops down, shots ring out, saber-slashes cut the air, resounding hooves trample the fleeing gypsies. Reality is reversed; now St. Joseph becomes a person and shrouds a fallen girl, the Virgin cures the wounded children. In that displacement typical of the Lorquian image, "Other lasses ran in flight,/Pursued by their tresses." Finally when all the roofs of the gypsy city "were furrows in the earth," the Guard went away through a "tunnel of silence," leaving the city in flames. Then in the last stanza García Lorca seizes the impact of the long poem and utilizes it personally by focusing the turmoil and persecution just described in his own face:

O ancient city of the gypsies,	(¡Oh ciudad de los gitanos!
Who can forget you soon?	¿Quién te vió y no te recuerda?
Let them look upon my face,	Que te busquen en mi frente.
Interplay of sand and moon.	Juego de luna y arena.)

These ballads of Antoñito el Camborio and of the Civil Guard, which show the theme of aggression leading to destruction, are, in our plan of discussion, the natural transition to the last two ballads of the book. In them the poet reaches death itself. In the "Ballad of the Summoned One," Lorca projects his figure of "The Embittered One" in a poem based on Spanish religious tradition. Lorca explained once (perhaps more poetically than factually) that he had felt himself to be the "Embittered One" ("*El Amargo*") since his boyhood, when he had been rejected or dominated crushingly by a boy about his age.[18] Along with this personal theme, Lorca evokes the religious tradition of being "summoned." For example, if even a king committed a heinous crime, by supernatural means he might be cited to die at a given time.[19] Lorca creates tension and mystery by emphasizing the punishment and leaving the crime obscure. Did he intend enigmatically to suggest his crime against society in this stanza, which has no clear relation to the other details of the ballad?

The massive oxen of the waters	(Los densos bueyes del agua
Surge around the lads,	embisten a los muchachos
Lads bathing in the crescent moons	que se bañan en las lunas
Of their undulating horns.	de sus cuernos ondulados.)

While much ink has been spilled identifying the Andalusian popular expression of the deep force of moving waters as oxen, the whole quatrain is a magnificent image of homosexual phantasy in the manner of the Whitman poem "Twenty-eight Young Men" in *Song of Myself.*

Except for this image, Lorca in his poem follows the details of the religious tradition. The poet's "loneliness without rest" is convincingly described, along with extended specific details of being cited: "Paint a cross upon the door/And put your name below,/For hemlock and the nettle sharp/Will from your body grow." Since the poem states that the period of grace granted before death is from June 25 until August 25, high summer, we assume that passion is connected with the crime. It is significant that the conclusion evokes the *Roman* tradition, associated in Lorca's mind with stoicism, uprightness and Roman Catholic tradition. In other words, the Embittered One dies sternly and firmly within the ancient Spanish tradition.

Men kept coming down the street	(Hombres bajaban la calle
To see the one unblest,	para ver al emplazado,
At work attaching to the wall	que fijaba sobre el muro
His loneliness at rest.	su soledad con descanso.
And there the spotless winding sheet	Y la sábana impecable
Of Roman accents cold,	de duro acento romano,
Gave an equilibrium to death	daba equilibrio a la muerte
With its well-squared folds.	con las rectas de sus paños.)

The other ballad with the theme of death that comes through frustration and persecution is the one numbered thirteen by Lorca and entitled "Dead from Love." Surely Lorca was aware of provoking confusion with this title. Whereas in all the other ballads the wild sexual passion is devoid of sentiment, in this one the title suggests the presence of a love intense enough to cause death. We are left uncertain, then, between ironic intent and a specialized personal meaning. The ballad draws heavily upon folk tradition. It is a time when the very earth is in upheaval: "What is that which casts a gloom/Along the hallways high?" The anonymous protagonist of the poem, sunk into bitter resignation, has retreated with the mother into the castle as midnight approaches. This kind of ominous scene had many variations in ancient folk poetry. Since suicide is possible but not suggested, we assume the sufferer is, as sometimes happens in the ancient folk poems, sickening unto death of love. Perhaps the ballad suffers from a lack of narrative direction. As an example of ultraistic effects at the end, the protagonist of the poem cautions his mother that when he dies she is to "send out blue telegrams/To South and to North." These last two ballads project Lorca's idea at this time that resignation through death is the only solution to the persecution which besets mankind.

In summary, the *Gypsy Ballads* is a book which reveals Federico García Lorca's unsurpassed imagination in transmuting the materials of Andalusian popular tradition into an expression of his own tragic outlook on life. The book lacks a sense of balance; it shows little affirmation of the spiritual values of mankind. But in spite of this serious limitation, the *Gypsy Ballads* projects with white-hot intensity the primeval life force (often expressed through the sexual) which is continually seeking expression. Lorca intended that the book should be Andalusian with all its tragic complexities. In actual fact, however, the poet at every moment manipulates his Andalusian figures like marionettes in the shadow of the tragic frustration to which he felt himself doomed. As is proper in lyric poetry, the poet and his creations become transmuted into a book which is a new reality. In English literature, A. E. Housman's *A Shropshire Lad* provides a meaningful comparison. Lorca and Housman both projected through the popular ballad tradition their profound disappointment with life and an evasive attack on their respective cultures. Housman was masterful in creating a pure lyric; Lorca, the more passionate figure of the two, employed his extraordinary ability with modern metaphor in creating an original poetic style. Both Housman and Lorca lived to see their books taken over as public property, with interpretations often contrary to their purpose. Lorca's *Gypsy Ballads*, which has gone through more than a dozen editions in Spanish, has attained the glory of being assimilated into the stream of modern European literature.

CHAPTER 4

Poet in New York (Poeta en Nueva York)

I Introduction to the Theme and Form

IN our view, *Poet in New York* is a logical continuation of the *Gypsy Ballads*, but with many significant changes. Basically the poet's problem is still the channeling of the physical instincts so that he can adequately express his life in his art. While in the *Gypsy Ballads* Lorca voiced his tragic frustration through traditional materials often associated with the gypsy, in *Poet in New York* he generally seeks to take off from direct experience, which is then transmuted into symbolic expression. Whereas the *Gypsy Ballads* are developed through narrative progression in which there are many abstruse images and metaphors, *Poet in New York* is almost completely in symbols, and these allow much latitude for interpretation. The ballad form gives way generally to free verse of loose rhythms. The egocentric attitude, more or less disguised in the former book, becomes exaggerated in the latter, descends to the point of no return and begins to change at the conclusion of the book. While in the earlier book the poet surrenders to the tragic frustration by projecting psychological defeat and death, in the latter he fights through to at least the beginnings of victory. Above all, Lorca speaks with the modern voice of alienation and rebellion and despair.

The poems of the *Poet in New York* are strong brew which many readers will prefer to dilute. Lorca, before an audience in Buenos Aires for a public reading of the book, arms himself like a Puritan divine preparing to wrestle with Satan: "I bring you a bitter and living poetry to lash your eyes open. . . . I want to wrestle with you, disturb you, belabor you, to fight you to a fall or be struck down in turn." [1] Obviously he is preparing the audience to expect a revolutionary kind of poetry. Moreover, it is of importance that while in New York he was preoccupied with Lautréamont's *Chants of Maldoror,* which he apparently took as a model.[2] Let us remember that Lorca printed only chosen poems from the book during his lifetime; although he arranged the text in 1935, *Poet in New York* was finally published in Mexico in 1940, with the American translation appearing in that same year.[3]

Poet in New York has a double theme, as Lorca himself analyzed it; the poet projects and attempts to resolve a crisis of the city as seething death-in-life and at the same time a crisis in his own life.[4] The symbol common to both is suffering. The point of contact between the city and the poet are New York's persecuted minorities, above all the Negroes. The book, said Lorca, is a meeting of "my poetic world with the poetic world of New York, extra-human architecture and furious rhythm, geometry and anguish." [5] The chronology of presentation of the poems follows the poet's own chronology of action: he arrives with his baggage of memories, has a strong encounter with himself and the city, withdraws to Vermont for a respite, returns changed to face the city, then departs. In the ten sections of the book, each of which includes several poems, he presents some of the most turgid, despairing, rebellious and ironically difficult poetry in Spanish literature.

II *The Poet's Encounter with Himself and the City*

The magnitude of the poet's crisis is made clear in the initial poem, "Back from a Walk," for he has been "Assassinated by heaven,/crushed between the forms which lead toward the serpent/and the forms which seek the crystal," that is, between the serpent of the flesh and the crystal of art.[6] In large part, the poet brought this crisis to New York with him, and the strange environment has served to exacerbate it. This section of poems bears as an epigraph a phrase from the younger poet Cernuda which stunningly fixes Lorca's present position looking backward: "Fury color of love/Love color of oblivion." The fury surely refers to the truncation of the artistic-personal attachment to Dalí; this theme, which some readers will prefer to ignore, is one which has a certain importance throughout the book.

In the other poems of this section the poet looks toward his past. In "1910" he recalls what seems a normal childhood, but in which finally "dream stumbled against reality." Then occurs the first of the poet's despairing statements in this book: "Ask me nothing else. I have seen that things/when they seek their course encounter the void." In the "Fable and Round of the Three Friends" the poet laments the separation from Enrique, Lorenzo and Emilio, who seem respectively a sort of Don Juan, a poor artist perhaps and a scholar. Significant is the fact that they "lost themselves weeping and singing for a hen's egg," that is, they died in domesticity. In the final poem of this section, the poet evokes "childhood, a fable of fountains now," that is the overflowing of innocence; this childhood is expanded to embrace love, "a childhood of ocean." Within this imagery of the power of memory, the poet, "with the grief of a hobbled Apollo," is going to pursue the spirit of Apollonian man, even against the fury of heaven.

In the second section of *Poet in New York* Lorca introduces us to the city through his picture of the Negroes of Harlem, and it is a tribute to his power that in just two poems he has created a "King" of such lasting impression. The first poem, "Norm and Paradise of the Negroes," is conceptually non-specific; the mass of symbols is not focused sharply. The paradise of the Negro is his love for "blue without history," that is, his innocence in physical expression uninhibited by morality and laws. "The King of Harlem" is an imaginary portrait of the Negro in his natural setting. The first lines of the long poem (it totals one hundred nineteen lines) have been widely quoted:

> With a spoon
> he was gouging out the eyes of crocodiles
> and thumping on the monkeys' behinds.
> With a spoon.

> (Con una cuchara,
> arrancaba los ojos a los cocodrilos
> y golpeaba el trasero de los monos.
> Con una cuchara.)

Not just wild imagination, here in this scene the Negro in his primitive innocence is daring to gouge out the eye, the point of contact between himself and the crocodile, a symbol of guilt and repression. The civilized white of course could not so happily suppress his guilt.

But Lorca emphasizes prophetically the pent-up violence in the Negro, the result of long persecution:

Blood has no outlets in your night face upward,
There is no blush. But blood is raging under the skin,
live in the thorn of a dagger and the breast of a landscape.

(La sangre no tiene puertas en vuestra noche boca arriba.
No hay rubor. Sangre furiosa por debajo de las pieles,
viva en la espina del puñal y en el pecho de los paisajes.)

This thwarted vitality has also become pent-up anguish in the Negro.

> There is no anguish equal to your flame-red oppression,
> to your blood perturbed under dark eclipse,
> to your garnet ferocity, deaf and dumb in the shadows,
> to your great imprisoned King, in a doorman's suit.
>
> (¡No hay angustia comparable a tus ojos oprimidos,
> a tu sangre estremecida dentro del eclipse oscuro,
> a tu violencia granate sordomuda en la penumbra,
> a tu gran rey prisionero con un traje de conserje!)

A summary can but poorly suggest the richness and elaboration of the imagery in this long poem, certainly one of the most powerful and artistically satisfying in the book.

In the section "Streets and Dreams," the first three poems present the heart of Lorca's view of the city as seething mass, movement without life, life-in-death. The "Dance of Death" is a modern version of a chilling superstition as old as the Middle Ages in Spain. The poet's view of the city is exaggerated almost beyond description. It is the time of the meeting of dead animals, "the eternal joy of the hippopotamus with hooves of ashes," when "the Chinaman wept on the roof/without finding the nude body of his wife" and the director of the bank was observing the manometer "that measures the cruel silence of money." This is the theme which finally emerges clearly: a denunciation of wealth. Death is pictured as a great masked figure which casts oblivion, guilt and fear over the city. And when "the cobras are hissing on the upper floors," the death-masked figure will arrive at the Stock Exchange, which will be a "pyramid of moss."

In "Landscape of the Vomiting Multitudes" the poet employs

the sub-human imagery of the surrealists (or the Freudians) to convey his horror of the seething masses and the meaninglessness of their movement. Apparently he saw no conflict between his point of view in this poem and that of the earlier ones which expressed sympathy for the Negroes of Harlem. He aptly chooses Coney Island at dusk as a background for a kind of scene predicted generally in Ortega y Gasset's *Revolt of the Masses*. The dominant figure in one chosen at the realistic level to express Lorca's personal antipathy: "The fat woman came walking along/ pulling up roots and wetting the parchment drumheads,/the fat woman/who turns the suffering octopus inside out . . ." This image of the fat woman and of vomit as signs of rejection and spleen pervade the short poem.

A companion piece to this poem is "Landscape of the Urinating Multitudes," subtitled a "Nocturne of Battery Place." Of more direct application to Lorca himself than the other "Landscape," this poem continues the dread sense of isolation but with a persistent thread of action. While men and women stand by unresponsively, a lad (*niño*) on a Japanese sailboat (the poet himself in alien surroundings) wails for help. The line "It matters not whether the lad stays quiet when they cleave him with the ultimate needle" is ambiguous in this poem; here the sense of rejection and lack of human concern are the themes which stand out.

The series of poems which follow presents the central part of the poet's crisis and his reaction to it; and while the critics have largely obscured the poems' meaning with the intention of protecting their author, they are very important in the structure of the book. The brief lyric "Murder," subtitled "Two Voices at Dawn on Riverside Drive," is a brief dialogue which on the surface describes a knifing. Lorca, with poetry more real to him than reality itself, insisted later that he *overheard* the conversation, but this is palpably untrue, because he would not have understood the English language. Since at the realistic level the poem presents a murder, we expect its symbolic meaning to be different. And, in this ambiguous imagery and suggestive dialogue, the poet seems to be presenting a homosexual "murder," as one speaker assaults the other.

The poem "Christmas on the Hudson," with Lorca's peculiar emphases, is a kind of re-expression of the Fall, a fall from a state of innocence to the practices of the flesh. Earlier in the book (in Section II), he had introduced the religious theme in "Abandoned Church." In this poem, a father laments the loss of a son who has lost himself playing "upon the ultimate stairways of the Mass." In "Christmas on the Hudson" the irony of the title soon becomes obvious, for although a spectral chorus is singing "Alleluia," the protagonist is in a cosmic isolation, "World alone in a heaven alone." This chorus can only be described as a mixture of the Dantesque and the surrealistic:

> The earthworm chanted a terror of wheels
> and the beheaded sailor
> chanted on the water-bear who was to stretch him out,
> and all were singing Alleluia,
> Alleluia. Heaven deserted. . . .

> (Cantaba la lombriz el terror de la rueda
> y el marinero degollado
> cantaba el oso de agua que lo había de estrechar;
> y todos cantaban aleluya,
> aleluya. Cielo desierto. . . .)

The poet changes from the elevated chant to a more intimate level, still with the emphasis on homosexual imagery (the sailors), finally coming to a conclusion: "What matters is this: void. World alone. Debouchment./Dawn, no. Lifeless Fable./Only this . . . Debouchment." The significant thing is that the "Fable of fountains," the innocence of his youth has been destroyed, and the poet is conscious only of the momentary pacification of the senses.

In "Dreamless City," subtitled with grim irony "Brooklyn Bridge Nocturne," there surge the awareness of guilt (or sin) and an emphasis upon the pressure of the flesh, of the physical senses. While no one sleeps, "The live iguanas arrived and set tooth on the dreamless men;/the heart-stricken . . . will meet on the corners/the mute incredible crocodile . . . " These animals are guilt symbols; Tennessee Williams in *The Night of the Iguana* was later to employ this creature in the same context. The poet chillingly becomes more personal, since the lad (*niño*) of the poem is of course Lorca himself: "And the lad they buried this morning was weeping so much/they had to call out the dogs to quiet him."

[84]

The passage which follows is of such importance for the poem that it must be quoted fully:

Life is no dream. Beware, beware, beware!
We fall down from the stairways to eat the humid earth,
or we climb to the snowy divide with the choir of dead dahlias.
But there is neither forgetfulness, nor dream:
Living flesh. Kisses tether our mouths
in a mesh of recent veins,
and whoever comes down to grief will grieve without rest,
and whoever fears death will carry it upon his shoulders.

(No es sueño la vida. ¡Alerta! ¡Alerta! ¡Alerta!
Nos caemos por las escaleras para comer la tierra húmeda
o subimos al filo de la nieve con el coro de las dalias muertas.
Pero no hay olvido, ni sueño;
carne viva. Los besos atan las bocas
en una maraña de venas recientes
y al que le duele su dolor le dolerá sin descanso
y al que teme la muerte la llevará sobre sus hombros.)

The first line lends a religious cast to the passage, since it suggests Calderón's famous play *Life is a Dream.* Calderón could staunchly deny the importance of the flesh and reduce physical existence on earth to a dream, for he could stand upon his solid Catholic faith in eternal rewards. Antonio Machado of the Generation of '98 was the first Spaniard to face this crisis of accepting life as a dream with only a weakened faith to support him. Lorca here is at the point of denying both dream and eternity; there is only the unbearable pressure of the living flesh. Even in his most intense moments, Lorca insists on being personal, for the suggestion of "dead dahlias" (*dalia*—Dalí) is unmistakable,[7] whether made consciously or unconsciously. For the moment, even his artistic inclinations have been stifled, but in the lines that follow he insists that on another day the roses of poetry will flow from his lips.

In "Blind Panorama of New York"—continuing in Section III—the poet in resignation is seeking to analyze his position. His inspiration (the birds of the poem) is gone for the moment, as is the little love he knew; he is tormented by the "desire for aggression" and the "metallic murmur of suicide." He is certain only that "The true anguish which keeps things in awareness/is a small infinite flame"; further on he calls it "a small space of air live to the mad fusion of light." But thus far the poet has not succeeded in keeping his eyes on the flame: "Often I have lost myself/in seeking the flame that wakens awareness of things,/and I have found only sailors cast upon the guardrails . . ." For now, he concludes, "Here only the Earth exists."

Lorca ends this section with two poems, both of which express hopelessness. "Dawn" is an ugly picture of daybreak in New York, where the black pigeons pick at the dead waters in "four pillars of slime." "Dawn comes, and there is no mouth to receive it," for in the whole city there is no hope, only "numbers and laws." The "Birth of Christ," with a night setting, is an outstanding example of the surrealist manner. The poet seems to be on the street at Christmas, perhaps near a church. At the beginning the poet is seeking help: "A shepherd gropes for the nipple in the drifting snow . . ." But Christ is presented as a little clay figure, with his fingers chipped off. Joseph is near the manger, but the poet sees also wolves and toads, mules and bulls, unstrung zithers and beheaded voices. The whole scene conveys no sense of life or hope to the poet, as his surrealist image suggests· "The swaddling clothes exhale a sound of desert." The "idiot priests" who vanish trailing after Luther among the high arcades suggest not an attack on Protestantism, but rather the poet's utter isolation; he is unable to respond at all to the traditional hope of Christianity.

III *Interlude in Vermont*

After the agony and desolation of the poems just discussed, we should hope for surcease in the sections of the book (IV and V) to follow; and indeed these sections are presented as an interlude while the poet is away from the city in rural Vermont. There has been a tendency to call these poems "bucolic," and to emphasize the soothing phrase affixed as an epigraph from the pastoral poet Garcilaso de la Vega: "Our flock is grazing, the breeze expires." Certainly for Lorca the phrase is grim irony. For while some of the turbulence of the previous poems is lacking, there is an agony, a desolation, a hopelessness, a dull spleen and a spiritual emptiness which pervades the very atmosphere. Perhaps in the last poem of section V the poet shows some sign of wishing to continue the struggle of life.

In "Double Poem from Lake Eden Mills" the poet presents threads of various themes. He begins with a lament for his past innocence, when "roses flowed from my lips," and "the grass did not know the impassive bite of the stallion," that is, the hunger of physical passions. He rejects for himself the normal existence of man: "Let me pass by that door/where Eve eats ants/and Adam fecundates dazzling fishes." What he seeks is liberty, and specifically his liberty to love, in the "darkest corner of the breeze." And in the tension of the struggle the poet's surrealist manner is put aside and for one of the few times in the book he breaks into pathetic direct statement:

> I want to cry because I just want to,
> as the schoolboys cry on the back benches,
> because I'm not a man, not a poet, not a leaf,
> but a wounded pulse that probes the things of the other side.

> (Quiero llorar porque me da la gana
> como lloran los niños del último banco,
> porque yo no soy un hombre, ni un poeta, ni una hoja,
> pero sí un pulso herido que sonda las cosas del otro lado.)

In "Heaven Alive" the poet as "wounded pulse" is seeking a new landscape, of love and nothingness, where "the truth of equivocated things is understood." But for now he must be content with a limited love: "I stumble reeling against hard fixed eternity/and at the end love without dawn. Love. Visible love!"

The poem "Little Boy Stanton" is so excruciatingly personal that even Schonberg passed it by as "paranoiac," but since Lorca had five years to contemplate publishing or destroying it, we feel it must have consideration. It begins with a dialogue in English: "Do you like me?"/"Yes, and you?"/"Yes, yes." The scene of the poem is dominated by a living cancer that prowls along the halls, howls like a dog, permeates the atmosphere and finally attacks the boy himself. In this lugubrious climate the poem's direction is fairly clear. The poet's anguish "was bleeding through the afternoon/when your eyes were two walls." Then these lines follow:

> My agony, gritty, chewed by curs,
> sought its own garment,
> and you followed it without trembling
> down to the door of dark waters.

(Mi agonía buscaba su traje
polvorienta, mordida por los perros,
y tú la acompañaste sin temblar
hasta la puerta del agua oscura.)

In short, there is a contemplated seduction of the boy. But the
poet, seeing "flowers of terror," sends the boy away to develop as
he himself has developed. Meanwhile, the poet will grimly abide:
"I'll be penetrating shoutingly green statues of Malaria."

In the poem starkly entitled "Cow," which was suggested by a
personal experience in the country, Lorca makes striking use of an
ancient symbol. What was in reality a sick cow, her muzzle froth-
ing with saliva, is soon transmuted into the symbol for feminine
fertility. "Cows, the living and the dead,/blush of light and honey
of stable/were bawling with half-opened eyes." Then comes an
attack on an individual lured by this fertility: "Then let the
roots be advised;/and yonder lad now whetting his knife,/that
the cow is ready to be eaten." As the poet watched, the cow,
hooves shuddering in the air, turned to ash, "and now went off
bawling/through the wastes of the dead heavens,/where the
drunken ones lunch on death." This psychological association of
normal female fertility as death, presented in the grimmest terms,
is an insistent motif in Lorca's mature work. We suspect he was
drawing on a recent event in the present poem. While Lorca and
Dalí had until 1928 elaborated anti-feminine sentiment together,
Dalí had recently betrayed Lorca's ideal by becoming overwhelm-
ingly attracted to a woman who became for him lover, wife, sister,
mother, Madonna and permanent refuge, as his perhaps too-frank
autobiography reveals.[8]

Following "Cow," Lorca returns to one of his important themes,
the repression of his vital passion, in "Lass Drowned in a Well,"
subtitled "Granada and Newburg." The well, in Lorca a symbol of
multiple meanings, can suggest the shackles of narcissism, a place
of self-destruction in its restricted waters or a binding repression
of vitality. Here the girl of the poem is a double of the poet, as the
subtitle suggests. (Newburg refers to the country retreat in Vermont where he wrote the poem.) The first lines declare that fear
of death causes less suffering than dammed-up vitality: "The eyes
of statues suffer from the darkness of the coffins/But the statues

suffer more from waters that have no outlet./That have no outlet."
And the poet continues with vague sketches of his conflicts, inter-
rupted after each two lines with the refrain, "Waters that have no
outlet." These waters, referring to the poet's vital passion with
emphasis on the sexual, can and should be projected on a larger
screen so as to suggest modern man's loss of vital direction.

It is surprising that the poems which continue the cycle written
during the interlude in Vermont (section VI) should be called
"Introduction to Death," since the ones we have been discussing
often touched the death theme. But thus it is, for "Death" is the
title of the first lyric. In it Lorca employs rapidly a progression of
the symbols we have come to expect in him to suggest the drive of
all things to become what they are not: The horse to become dog;
dog to be swallow; swallow, bee; bee, horse again. As we interpret
the symbols, things therefore follow a cycle from life force (the
horse) to corruption of the force to idealism to utility and back to
life force again. And this life force seeks to extract from the rose
(of life) its essence, but continually fails. Even the rose contains
not only light but also cries of alarm—the opposites of life. Finally
the poet himself is presented as a passionate seeker: "And I, along
the eaves,/what a seraph of flames I seek and am!" But, in spite of
his eager reaching, a "plaster archway," a barrier which perhaps
civilization and fate itself have constructed, dooms without effort
the striving of the poet. This is the "death" of the title of the
poem.

It is in the "Nocturne of the Void" that the poet reaches the
depths of despair in his feeling of isolation. The stanzas with a
grim collection of surrealist images record the agony of a lost love,
and the supreme agony is that the poet feels his own love weakening. What had been a clear image is dissolving in a sea of
faces: "Countenances grow impassively/in a diminished clamor of
grass." At the end of Part I of his poem, the poet, passion-driven,
threatens to seek other loves, finally concludes that all is gone. In
Part II, the poet is immovably centered within himself, his "void
transfixed with armpits broken." There is a reversal of normal
form: the reiterated personal pronoun "I" becomes the stanza, the
lines of disjointed images become the refrain. Perhaps there is a
glimmer of hope in the concluding words, signified by the horse's
color: "There is no new century nor recent light./Only a blue

[89]

horse and a dawn." The poem "Ruin" expresses again this relent-
less self-preoccupation, the poet "a wayfarer along his own white
torso," without finding a way out.

In "Landscape with Two Tombs and an Assyrian Hound," a
title which suggests a manner of surrealist painters, Lorca returns
to dialogue to project this scene of cosmic foreboding:
"Friend,/rouse yourself so you can hear the howl of the Assyrian
hound." This chilling howl penetrates to the heart of the chamber
and echoes where the cancer sleeps. Against the insistent theme of
many poems, "A long time I loved a lad," the howl finally brings
premonitions of death: "The howl/is a long purplish tongue that
leaves/ants of horror and liquor of lilies."

The transition poem between the retreat to the country and return to the city is the long and perplexing "Moon and Panorama
of the Insects," complete with another ironic epigraph, "Poem of
Love," this time from the Romantic poet Espronceda. Lorca begins with a burst of spleen by saying that if things are going well,
he is like a little girl, but if he is thwarted—and here he descends
to vulgar imagery—his heart is like a "lump of millenial bull-
dung." In subsequent lines the poet is answering the unasked
question about salvation. Salvation will not come from the saints
in the church windows, nor from the metaphysicians, nor from the
common man, nor from landscape poets. "All forms are lies."
What exists then? The memory of childhood (the cradle in the
attic), the insects and the moon. The creeping, devouring, milling
insects are the same seething, half-living, masses of men of the
earlier poems. The moon is that presence, tinged with death,
which witnesses the poet's sexual turmoil, in more general terms,
his "seeking of equilibrium." And why is this a poem of love? We
see only a massive irony in the subtitle. There is a ray of human
contact in the poet's hope that his struggle for equilibrium and his
restrained aggression "will alleviate the anguish of another de-
voured heart."

IV Return to the City

By the time García Lorca returns to the city he has recovered
command of himself and the will to continue the struggle. With a
more objective tone, in "New York" (Section VII) he sets himself
the task of seeking out the "river of turgid blood" (life) that

flows in the city. With unerring accuracy he focuses on the physical processes necessary for mass living. The trains of milk are endless. Every day there perish a million ducks and pigs and cows and sheep. And the wastes from all this slaughter clog the very rivers. These are the problems of "multiplication." But the poet, in a phrase reminiscent of Eliot, asks, "What shall I do, arrange the landscape?" No, he has come to denounce. Obviously Lorca has been caught up in the swirl of social ferment, the denunciation of the rich in favor of the poor, in the manner of John Steinbeck and so many others. He is going to denounce all those who are unaware of the "other half." This radical change from his intense self-concern and attacks on the masses earlier in the book is surprising but at least partly sincere; certainly Lorca has sensed a new direction in the affairs of the world.

Following this poem of social emphasis, Lorca attempted to focus specifically on large religious themes. "Jewish Cemetery," if we understand his purpose, presents the insufficiency of the Judeo-Christian tradition as a solution to the problems of man. Admittedly the poem is opaque, and most critics have ignored it. In the poem, the poet is in contemplation near the cemetery, which a Jew has just entered. The poet is there with his thirst for life, at the moment restrained, but showing its presence as "fever of jubilee," "celestial grass" and "green sunflowers." At the end his instincts are threatening to break loose: "Fevers of jubilee were dancing on humid cupolas." But in the body of the poem there is a wavering projection of the "Children of Christ" and the Jews and their influence. Under Christian influence man was at least somnolent: "The children of Christ were sleeping/and the water was a dove/and the wood was a heron/and the plummet was a hummingbird/and as yet the live prisons of fire/were consoled . . ." Meanwhile the persecuted sought to escape death by finding a scapegoat. But the Jew "was no port," his way of life was barren. In New York, however, the Jew "occupied the litter" of the Christians, that is, took their place, but the Jews could bring together as spirit only "half a dove." Finally, the Jew was left with only guilt and resignation, and "cut off his hands in silence." While this meditation is in the past tense, in the middle of the poem the poet in the present tense broke into this picture of Christians to announce a victim of their system: "The doctors put their scissors and their rubber gloves in the sterilizer/when the cadavers feel in their feet/the terrible brightness of another buried moon." Lorca is successful in conveying a certain impression of the guilt-plagued Jews, but he has attempted to embrace too much religious history to be convincing.

Next to "Jewish Cemetery," with its generalized religious implications, Lorca probably intended to place "Crucifixion," a personal poem of tremendous impact which has generally frightened away many critics.[9] It is not "buffoonery," as Schonberg has said; Lorca was capable of vicious irony directed at the cultured classes. "Crucifixion" traces the death-in-life of the poet alienated from both heaven and his fellow man. The people are still "vomiting on the street corners." And the poet's "blood" comes pouring down the mountain, filling his shoes; the angels are of no help, because "their chalices are of wind." From the South (Lorca's South of passion) come terrible cries: "The moon was burning with torches the phallus of the horses." Nearby a camel was weeping because he had "to pass through the needle's eye at dawn."

It seems to us that the juxtaposition of this religious image and the "burning phallus" is for Lorca eternal crucifixion, a thorn not in the flesh but the very bone: "Oh thorn nailed in the bone until the planets rust!" Then the Pharisees (as always, hypocrisy) offer their solution: "That accursed cow," which is in general feminine fertility, seems to be for Lorca that which engulfs and destroys man. As evening came, "the darkened city was agonizing under the hammerblows of the carpenters." But the poet is saved in a fashion:

> Known was the exact instant of the salvation of our life.
> For the moon washed with water
> the flame wounds of the horses
> and not the living girl-child they quieted in the sand.

> (Se supo el momento preciso de la salvación de nuestra vida.
> Porque la luna lavó con agua
> las quemaduras de los caballos
> y no la niña viva que callaron en la arena.)

This is apparently a baptism of the flesh (the girl-child is probably certain spiritual aspects of the poet), performed by the moon, both a sexual and a death symbol in Lorca. The poet is therefore crucified into life, a life where the Pharisees are still "kicking aside the drunkards and spitting salt of sacrifices/while the blood follows after them like the bleating of a lamb." This poem, of course in violation of Spanish Catholic tradition, is typical of the surrealist-Freudian period when what had been sanctified and hence forbidden themes were treated with the greatest familiarity.

After the prolonged agony of his struggle with the crisis of the directionless masses of New York and of his own personal crisis, García Lorca chose to cast his solutions in two odes (Section VIII). It is significant that there are two odes, for if he could have resolved his own problems in a total return to humanity and to the ancient ideals of Western Culture, he would have written only one, but obviously he was too honest to force a solution alien to his nature. The first of the odes, the "Cry toward Rome," is a clear expression of the coming rebellion of the masses against their leaders. Lorca's sympathy lies clearly with the masses. The "Ode to Walt Whitman," however, demands the most careful scrutiny to detect the poet's purpose and theme.

In the "Cry toward Rome," Rome as the seat of Christian culture, the poet imagines himself atop the high tower of the Chrysler Building. The ode becomes a series of prophetic denunciations. First, Lorca attacks the material and mechanical aspects of New York and of modern civilization. A mass of destructive elements will rain down on the tower itself, where nearby "a man is urinating on a dazzling dove," that is, where the spirit of man has been scorned. The poet tells us that in the city there are a million smiths and carpenters, who are making only chains and coffins for coming generations. Modern man in the city is unaware of "the mystery of the corn tassel," the tassel being a general symbol of life-giving connection with the Earth. More importantly, asserts Lorca, modern man has forgotten "that Christ can still provide the living water." He (and indeed his whole generation) had failed to find a living Christ, even in Spain. In a passage reminiscent of Yeats's poem "The Second Coming," Lorca declares that the leaders of men are preaching a gospel they no longer believe:

> The teachers instruct the children
> about a marvelous light that comes from the mount;

but what comes is a meeting of sewers
where the dark nymphs of anger raise a cry.

(Los maestros enseñan a los niños
una luz maravillosa que viene del monte;
pero lo que llega es una reunión de cloacas
donde gritan las oscuras ninfas del cólera.)

Lorca continues by saying that the leaders preach love and peace, but have it not; love is in the thirsting and oppressed masses.

The second part of the Ode is a ringing statement of the coming upheaval between the more fortunate half of society and the dispossessed masses:

The multitude, of hammer, violin and cloud, . . .
will raise a cry although brains splatter on the walls, . . .
will raise a cry before the towers, . . .
will raise a cry with heads covered with excrement, . . .
will raise a cry with such terrible voice
until cities tremble like little girls . . .
because we want to see fulfilled the will of the Earth,
which gives its fruits for all.

(La muchedumbre de martillo, de violín o de nube,
ha de gritar aunque le estrellen los sesos en el muro,
ha de gritar frente a las cúpulas, . . .
ha de gritar con la cabeza llena de excremento, . . .
ha de gritar con voz tan desgarrada
hasta que las ciudades tiemblen como niñas . . .
porque queremos que se cumpla la voluntad de la Tierra
que da frutos para todos.)

Perhaps there is a faint ring of propaganda in the lines, but in the six remaining years of his life Lorca was beginning to experience some of the spirit of this ode. And certainly his prophecy of social upheaval has been amply fulfilled.

The position of the "Ode to Walt Whitman" following the "Cry toward Rome" and its greater length—it has 142 lines—indicate its importance in the structure of the book. If our thesis that these odes are Lorca's concluding words on the double crisis in the life of the city and the poet is correct, then the Whitman ode is of supreme importance for Lorca and our understanding of him. Undoubtedly Lorca never understood the total structure of Whitman's *Leaves of Grass*, but he recognized in the American a kindred spirit, as the "Ode" demonstrates. The critics generally have not grappled seriously with the perplexing problems it presents. But Luis Cernuda has stated emphatically the poem's importance: "Perhaps the 'Ode to Walt Whitman' is the very heart of the book, at least in it the poet [Lorca] voices a sentiment which was the very reason for his existence and his work." Cernuda is also aware of a confusion: "To one who knew Lorca well, the effect of the 'Ode' is one of certain unfinished sculptures because the block of marble had a crack." [10]

In the beginning lines, while ordinary men "were struggling with industry," Lorca evokes the memory of the physical presence of the American poet. He has been continually aware of Whitman: "beautiful old man like the mist/who raised a cry like a bird/with its sex pierced by a needle." Whitman's dream is summarized in a later stanza:

> You were seeking a nude figure that was like a river,
> bull and dream that would join the wheel with the alga,
> father of your agony, camellia of your death,
> that would moan in the flames of your secret equator.

> (Tú buscabas un desnudo que fuera como un río,
> toro y sueño que junte la rueda con el alga,
> padre de tu agonía, camelia de tu muerte,
> y gimiera en las llamas de tu ecuador oculto.)

These lines, which of course project Lorca's dream also, suggest an exclusive masculine comradeship, a joining together in physical union and in artistic endeavor, as suggested by the symbols of alga and wheel. Lorca reinforces this intention in the concluding lines, where his rebellion against Western culture breaks out clearly, for he wants a "little Negro boy to announce to the gold-seeking whites/the arrival of the reign of the corn tassel." These lines are admittedly ambiguous, since the corn tassel (*espiga*) is often a general fertility symbol, but we feel that Lorca is using *espiga* in the phallic sense. Therefore, we suggest that his announcement of the "arrival of the reign of the corn tassel" is an echo of Whitman's proclamation of "the institution of the dear love of comrades."

Now this dream of Lorca's seems to us more suggestive of death than the acceptance of the normal continuity of life through the union of man and woman, but Lorca goes on to say that it is proper for man not to wait for posterity, that "there are bodies which ought not to be repeated in the dawn." Certainly he realizes that he is pursuing a route toward death, for he immediately breaks into what surely are his most despairing lines:

> Agony, agony, dream; ferment and dream.
> This is the world, my friend, agony, agony.
> The dead are decomposing under the clock of the cities, . . .
> and life is not noble, nor good, nor sacred.

> (Agonía, agonía, sueño, fermento y sueño.
> Este es el mundo, amigo, agonía, agonía.
> Los muertos se descomponen bajo el reloj de las ciudades, . . .
> y la vida no es noble, ni buena, ni sagrada.)

A large part of the poem is given to a diatribe against the "fairies" of the cities. The poet, preferring not to raise his voice against the "lad who writes the name of his lass on his pillow," that is, normal man, lashes out against the inverts of the streets, the "*pájaros*" of Havana, the "*jotos*" of Mexico, etc. Apparently the poet attacks them for surrendering to mere physical drives, devoid of any emotional or artistic attachment. The details contradict in part certain of the earlier poems in the book. We can say only that Lorca revealed later his hatred for the inverts who were "slaves of women," while of course retaining his dream of the ideal comrade.[11] In this ode to Whitman, it seems that Lorca was trying splenetically to force the reader into the world of his agony of confusion.

V Flight from the City

After these major odes, the poet is ready for the "Flight from New York." This section (IX) has the subtitle "Two Waltzes toward Civilization." Critics have misread the irony of this subtitle, "toward Civilization." In actual fact, could Lorca seriously contend that Spain was more "civilized" than New York? The poet probably intends to suggest that the freedom of expression he has experienced in New York will be forbidden by the restrictions of "civilization" in his native Spain. The important poem of this section is the "Small Viennese Waltz," a sarcastic play with many of the surrealist tricks. As critics have said, the poet has recovered his poetic rhythm, the poem being in a waltz tempo, but the rhythm is used to recall a love now become flippancy. For "Vienna" we should perhaps read "Paris," where Dalí was. The waltz and the lost love die together. And mixed among the lines that seem to be about "old lights of Hungary" comes the shock of a homosexual image in the concluding stanza that Lorca's admirers may well find unworthy of him.

The concluding poem of the book is a Cuban "*Son,*" a primitive Negro rhythm, written as the poet was stopping in Cuba on his journey home. Lorca catches the rhythm of the bongo drums:

> Whenever the full moon comes I'm off to Santiago, Cuba,
> I'm off to Santiago
> In a coach of dark water.

> (Cuando llegue la luna llena, iré a Santiago de Cuba,
> iré a Santiago
> en un coche de aguas negras.)

But as Schonberg has pointed out, this is no simple rhythmic exercise, for the poet's baggage is a series of difficult images and symbols. He is going with "the blond head of Fonseca," his passion is burned out, his fountain dry; "with the rose of Romeo and Juliet," a reference to his drama *The Public* dealing with the confusion over Juliet's sex; with "breeze and alcohol on the wheels," his work clouded; with a "harp of live trunks. Crocodile. Flower of tobacco," that is, pressure of live passion, continued guilt, and (perhaps) a childhood memory of his father. The concluding lines are pessimistic, for "the sea is drowned in sand," the sand being his symbol for barrenness. From these concluding poems, then, while we can say that Lorca has recovered his poetic rhythms, and some sense of objectivity, the themes demonstrate that he has fought through to the vision of a victory. Although the victory involves the acceptance of tragedy and disillusionment, the poet has conceived a program and is apparently determined to continue the struggle.

VI Conclusions

The critical reception of the *Poet in New York* has been extremely varied. When the poems started to appear, many Spanish critics, sure that Lorca was a popular poet, tended to regard the poetry from the New York period as a temporary aberration on his part. A faithful surrealist like Juan Larrea has preached that Lorca threw himself into a trance, became a real seer and evoked in the book the chaos of the Spanish Civil War and the poet's own death.[12] There has been a strong tendency to extract the piquant details about the Harlem Negroes, the ringing denunciation of the rich and the promise of the future for the poor. Only a few commentators, such as Schonberg, have pointed out Lorca's insistence, unusual for a Spaniard, on presenting shocking and thus far prohibited themes. Far too many critics (even Americans like William Carlos Williams) have over-stressed the tired theme of New York as "mechanical" America, for who can deny that the creation of the great city of New York and her modern symbols demanded outstanding vision and imagination?

In summary, *Poet in New York* is a book like the serpent, half fascinating and half repulsive to the reader, but with a consistent intensity. Strongly within the surrealist tradition, it is an outstanding example of the almost exclusive use of symbols in conveying poetic meaning. It is also an achievement in poetic form. *Poet in New York* can be meaningfully compared with Lautréamont's *Chants de Maldoror* and Rimbaud's *A Season in Hell*, both written earlier than the surrealist period but achieving their importance during that period. *Poet in New York* begins as its own kind of season in Hell and ends with a somewhat shabby victory; probably Lorca's book has greater intensity than Rimbaud's, especially in individual poems. Like the *Chants of Maldoror*, in its demands for liberty, *Poet in New York* implies an attack on social and religious institutions, although, as we have seen, the poet himself tried to divide his allegiance. But Lorca's book, more individual and never totally rebellious, avoids the sense of contrived hysteria and studied decadence of Lautréamont's. *Poet in New York* is a painful, tormented, prophetic book, worthy of being included among the finest examples of the alienation of spirit in modern man.

CHAPTER 5

The Later Poetry

I Divan of Tamarit (Diván del Tamarit)

AFTER returning to Spain from New York, perhaps as early as 1931 Lorca began the creation of the lyrics that became the slim volume *Divan of Tamarit*, finally published in 1940. The *Divan* (Arabic word for gathering, by extension, anthology) and the Tamarit (a place near Granada) in the title suggest a specific evocation of the Arabic civilization. After a long period during which scholars such as Menéndez y Pelayo grounded Spanish cultural tradition almost completely in Greco-Roman and Western Christian origins, gradually Spanish scholars began to explore the influence of the Arabic culture. Lorca, not a scholar indeed, but sensitive to living influences, was, by general critical agreement, attracted to a book of Emilio García Gómez, *Arabigoandalusian Poems*, published in 1930. This anthology, with a fine prologue, contains in prose translation a sampling of poetry written in Arabic in Andalusia during the years 1050–1250.

In reading these poems, Lorca undoubtedly felt a spiritual kinship with the Arabic poets. There is in them a sense of lonely isolation, a feeling of resignation and futility. In spite of the occasional sensuality, even their love poems show a joy tinged with sadness. The poets' intense focus on individual elements (a lance, for example, or a horse) probably indicates a self-absorption, a retreat from life. Poetically, Lorca in this period was feeling age and lonely isolation and resignation. And in his Andalusia he could look back, not only down the long years of Spanish decline, but also down those agonizing years of the decay of the Arabic civilization in Spain. García Gómez has written a moving passage on those years, with special words for poetry. "After so many centuries of empire, Arabigoandalusian poetry, worked by infinite hands with so much grace . . . , was a globe that floated in the air, perhaps now without direction but charged with sensuality, swollen and tense with images, with perfumes and music. It could not resign itself to confinement in dusty manuscripts." [1] In his *Divan of Tamarit*, we shall see that from among the common Arabic themes—love, wine and orgy, battle, praise of the ruler, vignettes of nature, political satires—Lorca chose to concentrate on certain aspects of the Arabic love themes. It is significant, as García Gómez makes clear, that in the mature Arabic literary culture, three distinct themes of love existed. Naturally there was the sensual love of the harem beauty. There was also a kind of Platonic love, where the sensual is transmuted into artistic or divine love. Finally there was "Greek love," that system in which the poet extols the beauty and attraction of young lads, often of humble station in life. While Lorca ignores the first of these, it is fairly clear that in the *Divan of Tamarit* he projects a form of Greek love, sometimes with Platonic overtones.

The theme of the *Divan of Tamarit*, then, centers around the anguish of the memory of love and the poet's present despair, which he is struggling to transmute into poetry. The poet's voice has seemingly become disembodied, as Díaz-Plaja has said; his is a universe of presentiment and nostalgia, of dark instincts and faded passions. [2] The poet is able to draw upon the physical presence of the Arabic civilization which still exists in Spain as well as the literary motifs just discussed. Lorca calls twelve of the poems *Ghazals* (in Arabic a short lyric form usually with the theme of love) and the remaining nine poems he terms *Qasidas*. The Arabic *Qasida* was a longer poem of varied elements, one of these being the elegiac reminiscence of love or parting. Although in Arabic the *Qasida* tended to be more abstract, Lorca made no real distinction between the two forms. In the *Divan*, time hangs heavy so that the poems also suggest those of Antonio Machado, which have generally been called existential, in the sense of being frozen in time, of having no way out, of merely grimly enduring. Moreover, in the *Divan* there are flashes of surrealist irony and difficult evasions, couched in Lorca's personal images and metaphors. Finally, there is a threatening desperation which the poet keeps tightly controlled.

The initial lyric, *"Ghazal* of Unforeseen Love," which is extremely personal, is probably the key poem of the book. In it, Lorca sketches in imagery partly Oriental and partly surrealist his attraction to the comrade:

> No one understood the perfume
> Of your belly's dark magnolia.
> No one knew that you were martyring
> A hummingbird of love between your teeth.
>
> (Nadie comprendía el perfume
> de la oscura magnolia de tu vientre.
> Nadie sabía que martirizabas
> un colibrí de amor entre los dientes.)

The strange image of the "hummingbird of love" also appears in a painting of Dalí. Lorca's central image is the magnolia, which he has made dark with all the suggestion of *oscuro* for him—the dark night of passion, the *Sonnets of Dark Love,* dark as isolation and oblivion. The poet tried with all his being to make his love eternal, but even the broken stanza declares it was not to be:

> I sought to give you from my breast
> the letters cut from ivory that mean *forever,*
>
> *Ever, ever:* garden of my agony. . . .
>
> (Yo busqué, para darte, por mi pecho
> las letras de marfil que dicen *siempre,*
>
> *siempre, siempre:* jardín de mi agonía. . . .

Lorca is writing in the garden of Tamarit, the same one in which the Arabic poets mused long ago, but it has become for him a "garden of agony."

Having established this theme of brief love and separation in the first *ghazal,* Lorca goes on to explore aspects of memory, many of which are of course related to earlier poems. In "*Ghazal* of the Terrible Presence" the poet demands for the earth ominous supernatural happenings, that "water remain without channel," the wind without valleys, night without eyes, and that "the earthworms die from shadow." Ultimately the couplets contrast the foreboding cosmic and the personal: "Leave me in a frenzy of darkened planets/but show me not the freshness of your waist." The "*Ghazal* of Desperate Love" is a mixture of the turgid imagery of the New York poems and a refrain of Baroque preciosity: "Night wants not to come/so that you come not/nor can I go." Even the "*Ghazal* of Marvelous Love" ends in bitter defeat. "With all the chalk/of the evil earth/you were a reed of love, a dewy jasmine," the poet begins, but soon heaven and earth "were knotting chains in his hands," then the doubled heavens were flagellating his wounds. In the sparse couplets of the "*Ghazal* of the Remembrance of Love" the poet is clinging to memory, for in a refrain reminiscent of Antonio Machado he again contemplates self-destruction: "A wall of evil dreams/separates me from the dead." The "*Ghazal* of the Bitter Roots" suggests a persistent Lorquian theme amplified elsewhere in his work. Lorca found these "bitter roots" in the heart of all mankind, but especially in his own. In his lyric he sullenly strikes out at both love and man's life force: "Love, enemy mine, bite your bitter roots."

One of the more meaningful lyrics is the "*Ghazal* of the Dead Lad," an image of many evocations for Lorca. It can mean the loss of childhood innocence, the repression of childhood vitality and self-expression and the innocence of adolescent love. In this poem the dead one wavers between being poet and the beloved. One of the stanzas has a tragic beauty in the freshness of the whole image pattern, even in translation.

> The dead are bearing wings of moss.
> The misty wind and the limpid wind
> are two pheasants flying around the towers,
> and the day is a wounded lad.

> (Los muertos llevan alas de musgo.
> El viento nublado y el viento limpio
> son dos faisanes que vuelan por las torres
> y el día es un muchacho herido.)

The imagery becomes more exaggerated in the surrealist manner in the last stanza:

A water-giant descended on the mountain
and the valley went rolling with hounds and lilies.
Your body, with the violet shadow of my hands
was an archangel of ice, dead by the river.

(Un gigante de agua cayó sobre los montes
y el valle fué rodando con perros y con lirios.
Tu cuerpo, con la sombra violeta de mis manos,
era, muerto en la orilla, un arcángel de frío.)

In three of the *Ghazal* poems Lorca returns to motifs and popular forms of his earlier years, but still with emphasis on his own
peculiar view of the world. The "*Ghazal* of a Love that Hides its
Face" draws upon a popular tradition of Granada, whereby on
the second of January the girls have the bells in the tower of the
Vela ring to assure their finding a sweetheart during the year.
Lorca's stanza is like a popular song: "And when I heard/the bells
in the Vela tower/I put on your crown of verbena." Granada was
for the poet "a moon/drowned in the ivy," that is, as he usually
saw the city, ancient and sometimes moribund. Then, having established the joyful tradition of the bells, Lorca crushes it by suggesting the confusion of the identity of the lover: "I was consum-
ing myself in your body/without knowing whose it was."

The "*Ghazal* of Love with a Hundred Years" is a return to the
ultraistic manner of *Songs* and a variation on the theme of the
disappearing horsemen of the *Cante jondo*. There is a succession
of scenes, punctuated by the tragic Andalusian refrain, "Ay."

Four gallant lads   (Suben por la calle
Go up the street.   los cuatro galanes.

Ay, ay, ay, ay.   *ay, ay, ay, ay.*)

Then three gallants come down the street, then two, who come
together, only to become one gallant and the air. Finally there is
nobody, who is pacing up and down almost as real as the gallants.

The "*Ghazal* of the Morning Market" has the brisk popular
rhythms and a tragic refrain which tend to obscure the impact of
interspersed images persistent in Lorca. The refrain, actually stylized in the artistic Spanish heptasyllable, recalls the old ballad of

Reconquest days, when the Moorish King was pacing from one gate to the other:

Through old Elvira's arch	(Por el arco de Elvira
I want to see you go;	quiero verte pasar,
I want to learn your name	para saber tu nombre
And sit me down in woe.	y ponerme a llorar.)

While the poet looks backward, his thoughts become embittered; and, as Cernuda rightly suspected but would not insist upon, the images such as "needle of cactus short" become obscene to the normal person.[3] The word "market" in the title is used in the poem to indicate ironically the poet's betrayal by the lover, now singing an alien tune: "What voice for my punishment/You raise in the markets!"

The *Divan of Tamarit* has a brief collection of nine *Qasidas*. These poems are some of Lorca's most profound lyrics, especially if we read them as a final statement on his insistent themes. Chiefly of two types, the larger group states his present personal position, a kind of cosmic resignation; the second group, a promising treatment of symbols like the rose in a more abstract poetry. It is obvious that Lorca was beginning to transcend the too-personal note of some of the poetry of early maturity, but of course his tragic death cut short this development.

In the initial "*Qasida* of the Lad Wounded by Water" Lorca returns to the symbolic well and the walls of his Granada, a Granada of personal loneliness. His ever-returning symbols are here, but with new power and freshness. There is the eternal conflict of the life-force and nothingness:

The wounded lad wept moaningly,	(El niño herido gemía
His head with hoar-frost crowned;	con una corona de escarcha.
Pools and cisterns and fountains all	Estanques, aljibes y fuentes
In the air brandished swords.	levantaban al aire sus espadas.
What deserts of light were sinking low	¡Qué desiertos de luz iban hundiendo
The sand-wastes of the dawn!	los arenales de la madrugada!
The lad was all alone	El niño estaba solo
With the city asleep in his throat.	con la ciudad dormida en la garganta.)

Then face to face with his anguish, the poet falls extended along the earth, his agony curving over him. And he wants to die his death "by great mouthfuls," a death of cosmic frustration. This poem, read in proper chronological sequence at the end of his production, is one of the most deeply moving Lorca ever wrote, especially if taken with the two which follow.

The "*Qasida* of Lamentation," which Gerardo Diego extracted for his well-known anthology, is a frenzied dirge which achieves its impact not by repetition but by conciseness. Although the poet closes his balcony, the sounds of lamentations echo unceasingly behind the "gray walls." Within his consciousness few angels sing, few hounds bark and a thousand violins fit in the palm of his hand (that is, his poetic voice has sunk to nothing). But as the lamentation surrounds the poet it becomes inextricably mixed with his confused emotions:

But the lament is an immense hound,	(Pero el llanto es un perro inmenso,
the lament is an angel immense,	el llanto es un ángel inmenso,
the lament is an immense violin, . . .	el llanto es un violín inmenso . . .)

And the sound of the lamentation is heard in all the land.

The "*Qasida* of the Branches" continues the series of lyrics with deep personal implications. The poet, seated in his "garden" of Tamarit, is contemplating the late autumn afternoon:

Along the pathways of the Tamarit have come the hounds with leaden feet	(Por las arboledas del Tamarit han venido los perros de plomo
to await the falling of the branches,	a esperar que se caigan los ramos,
to await the breaking of the lonely boughs.	a esperar que se quiebren ellos solos.)

As Guillén has commented,[4] instead of the simple image of the falling leaves, the poet projects the fall of the branches themselves. But we fail to understand why Guillén finds this poem "elegant." As Lorca would say, the poem is hard and bitter in his throat, and it has his usual puzzling complexities. For in subsequent lines the heavy branches become "joyful," although dusk is coming "with elephant tread." In the enigmatic final stanza, there is an evocation of the persistent image of the "lads with inscrutable faces." Therefore, with the lads, the poet and the branches (which in the rare masculine form *ramos* here would seem to have sexual connotations), Lorca has persisted in the personal emphasis we have come to expect of him.

As a conclusion to this series of personal lyrics, Lorca in the "*Qasida* of the Impossible Hand" chooses a frank simplicity of expression to state a quiet resignation. Was he perhaps echoing a line from Rimbaud's *Season in Hell* in calling for human aid?

I want no more than a hand,	(Yo no quiero más que una mano,
a wounded hand if it can be.	una mano herida, si es posible.
I want no more than that hand	Yo no quiero más que esa mano
for daily ablutions and the white	para los diarios aceites y la
sheet of my agony.	sábana blanca de mi agonía.)

"The rest all passes," he says; the rest is only a "sad wind," the same sad wind which ends the *Lament for the Death of a Bullfighter*. Schonberg has suggested that "The Impossible Hand" was inspired by a poem of Mutamit with Platonic (or spiritual) theme; we believe that the human emotion it conveys is sufficient.

In the final *Qasidas* Lorca is beginning to work with a more abstract symbolism. Certainly he did not have to leave the Arabigoandalusian poems to find models, for the poets of the Arabic civilization had developed extensively a pattern of human-toward-divine inspiration something like Platonism, which utilized the conventional symbols of wine, dove, etc. Lorca's "*Qasida* of the Reclining Woman" seems a transition toward abstraction. As he first contemplates the nude woman, she is a "pure form," a form closed toward the future. The rest of the poem is Lorca's restatement of the inferior feminine as fertility without "light," that is, spirit, feminine fertility expressed in ugly terms of death:

Your belly is a struggle of roots,	Tu vientre es una luncha de raíces,
and your lips a formless dawn.	tus labios son un alba sin contorno,
Below the lukewarm roses of the bed	Bajo las rosas tibias de la cama
moan dead men awaiting turn.	los muertos gimen esperando turno.

The "*Qasida* of the Rose" is Lorca's attempt to express with the ancient symbol of the rose that ideal goal sought by the poet, the center of being, the ultimate aim of his work. For Lorca, the rose is not dawn or future promise; neither is it the clarity of science or the shadow of nothingness. Fixed, almost eternal, the rose is a "confine of flesh and dream." And what is the rose seeking? Lorca is enigmatic; it is seeking, or has sought—the poem is in the past tense—"something else." We assume that Lorca intends for us to search for his rose in all his work, and there is an implied uncertainty in the poet's mind in regard to the mystery of life.

The "*Qasida* of the Golden Girl" is even more enigmatic, but we believe it traces the history of the poet's emotional and therefore his poetic development; the changes in the girl express the poet's changing inspiration. The lyric is thus in the same vein as Jiménez' "Poetry," a famous statement of the three stages of his poetic development. Of course the development of the symbol of the girl in Lorca's poem indicates that his poetic development was different from that of Jímenez. In his adolescence, Lorca's inspiration was pure:

The golden lass	(La muchacha dorada
bathed in the waters	se bañaba en el agua
and the waters became golden.	y el agua se doraba.)

When the "algae and branches" appeared (sexual reality), the girl became white; that is, not purity necessarily, but of reduced importance. Under increased pressure of vitality or sexuality, the "dripping girl" of inspiration is almost lost in the flaming waters of sexuality. When dawn came with a "thousand bovine faces" (reality), inspiration was frozen, inert. Then "the lass in tears/bathed among flames/and the nightingale cried/with burned wings." Now inspiration has been consumed in the flames of sexual reality. Finally the girl as inspiration becomes another symbol, the white heron; this probably suggests to Lorca unattainable fantasy: "The golden lass/was a white heron/and the water gilded her." Of course explanation can convey little of Lorca's remarkable achievement in musicality and ample poetic suggestion with such economy of expression.

The book ends with the "*Qasida* of the Dark Doves," one of

those Lorquian lyrics which seem both infantile and overmature at the same time. Dedicated to Jorge Guillén's son Claudio, very young as Lorca remembered him, the poem displays a number of the basic symbols, but has as its theme nothingness. The two dark doves become sun and moon, the great duality of matter and spirit, masculine and feminine. When the poet asks his destiny, both doves claim him, but the poet now sees two "snowy eagles" and a lass. Then we find out that "The one was really the other/and the lass she was none." Finally, the poet sees among the laurel "two bare doves," but of these also "The one was really the other/and the two they were none." In this playful tone, is Lorca predicting nothingness for body and spirit, and even the disappearance of his poetic symbols? More than once Lorca's avowed aim was to leave the reader perplexed over the intricacies of his art.

It is difficult to reach a final conclusion as to the value of *Divan of Tamarit* as a book in relation to Lorca's poetry. Certainly as a group these lyrics are among the most profound and concise Lorca ever wrote. With his usual poetic intuition he appropriated a rich field of suggestion, the literary and historical world of the Arabic civilization, but as usual retained his own personal emphases and forms. He displayed a mature mastery of a number of traditional poetic lines, employed in a variety of arrangements, so that the effect is a fine balance between freedom of form and control of it. There is, however, the extreme brevity of the book, caused in part by Lorca's persistent unconcern with manuscripts. For example, a fine lyric called "Song of the Diminutive Death," written in the same period and printed separately, would have strengthened the *Qasida* section. Moreover, in a general sense, this book has perhaps too few new themes to stand apart from Lorca's earlier poetry, although some of the poems of the *Divan* indicate that he was ready to explore new areas, probably with more objectivity. In spite of some shortcomings, in conjunction with the major books *Gypsy Ballads* and *Poet in New York*, the *Divan of Tamarit* stands as a powerful and logical conclusion to a critical epoch in his life and work.

II   Lament for the Death of a Bullfighter
(Llanto por Ignacio Sánchez Mejías)

It is fitting that Lorca's last important poem should be the *Lament for the Death of a Bullfighter,* for in this noble elegy the poet succeeded in interweaving many significant aspects of Spanish tradition, while at the same time he demonstrated his own personal and poetic qualities. Springing from direct experience as did most of Lorca's poems, the elegy was written soon after the death in the ring of the Sevillian bullfighter, Ignacio Sánchez Mejías. On August 11, 1934, Sánchez was severely gored in Manzanares; transferred to Madrid, he died two days later. Lorca finished the poem by early November, read it at a performance of his drama *Yerma* in early 1935, and published it in the same year.

Sánchez Mejías, of eminent reputation as a bullfighter, was also a man of solid intellectual interest and achievement. Married to the sister of the *torero* Joselito, he was appearing at *corridas* with Ortega and the famous Juan Belmonte by the time of his death. Sánchez Mejías firmly impressed Ernest Hemingway with his raw courage and skill, although the author of *Death in the Afternoon* felt that this bravery was expressed too boastfully. But Sánchez Mejías also had cultural interests which set him apart from the typical bullfighter, who was often an unlettered and superstitious gypsy blessed with natural grace and courage. In 1927 Sánchez Mejías organized a celebration for the Góngora Centennial in Seville, which Lorca and the poets of the Generation of 1927 attended. Surprisingly he also wrote and had produced in 1928 a full-length play called *Unreason* (*Sinrazón*), a believable drama of a doctor in the practice of Freudian psychiatry. At the point of curing a girl suffering from delusions that she is a queen, the doctor is killed by an aide, who insists that sweet delusions are preferable to grim reality.

Lorca was of course aware of the significance of the bullfight in Spain, but was strangely lukewarm in his reactions to it. In 1930, he declared in a lecture that "Spain is the only country where death is the national spectacle." He recognized that the bullfighter has to create a form of plastic art in the very presence of aggressive death, and that to retain grace and courage under these conditions is the real bullfighter's challenge. Now it is strange that

Lorca, supposedly a poet of death, had never utilized the bullfight in his work. We believe, as suggested before, that for Lorca death had been largely a metaphor, meaning the death-in-life, the hopeless frustration emphasized by the surrealists. Sánchez Mejías, in performing his art, had been seeking death, but the sense of finality when it came shook Lorca to his innermost being. This sense permeates the *Lament*.

The *Lament* is generally in the tradition of the classical elegy, as Calvin Cannon[5] has demonstrated in a sensitive article. And many critics have made minor comparisons between Lorca's poem and the most famous elegy in Spanish literature, Jorge Manrique's "Stanzas on the Death of His Father" ("Coplas por la muerte de su padre"), written in the 15th century, especially since a few stanzas of Lorca's are patterned after Manrique's. However, Lorca's individuality asserts itself even from the title. For Lorca, *lament* (*llanto*) would suggest personal emotion; *elegy*, a literary form. The elegy follows the usual pattern: the initial expression of grief in the presence of death, some recognition of the universality of death, praise of the departed one, philosophical speculation on death and a promise to immortalize the memory of the departed friend. The elegy is divided into four parts, or movements, each in a different stanzaic form. Many have called the poem a musical form such as the sonata, although it lacks allegro movements.

In the first section, "The Goring and Death," the poet gives way to horror and deep despair at the sudden arrival of death. An entirely modern scene, there is no sylvan bower or solemn chamber in which the fallen one lies. The projection of the scene itself is as if the poet had sharply fixed it in his mind, with sombre light focused on the terrible horn wound, only to have the scene disintegrate into individual elements, suspended without order. In the literary form of the section, however, a pattern is achieved by the alternating of classical hendecasyllables, which carry the imagery, and the octosyllabic refrain "At five in the afternoon," which helps to create the effect of a monotonous dirge.

At five in the afternoon.	(A las cinco de la tarde.
It was striking five in the afternoon.	Eran las cinco en punto de la tarde.
A boy brought the spotless sheet	Un niño trajo la blanca sábana

At five in the afternoon.	*a las cinco de la tarde.*
A pail of quicklime waiting near	Una espuerto de cal ya prevenida
At five in the afternoon.	*a las cinco de la tarde.*
The rest was death and only death	Lo demás era muerte y sólo muerte
At five in the afternoon.	*a las cinco de la tarde.*)

From the surrealist imagery like that of *Poet in New York* emerge the elements of the static scene. Death struggles with the bullfighter's body and spirit (symbolized by the leopard and dove respectively) while the spectators wait: "On the streetcorners groups of silence." The imagery is largely of the clinic, of cotton, oxide and arsenic, and the whole bullring is inundated in iodine. The wound is a "thigh with a desolate horn," "a trumpet of lilies in the greenish groin," while "In the distance gangrene comes." The insistence on the wound indicates modern man's rebelliousness at feeling himself deprived of life. Finally, "Death put eggs in the wound," and the bull, now the symbol of death itself, "was bellowing in his forehead." Even though this scene is short, Lorca is at his most powerful in the projection of the foreboding.

In the second section of the poem, "The Spilled Blood," the poet violently rejects the loss of life, then proceeds to a eulogy of the bullfighter and his courage. The blood in Lorca's poetry is the symbol of man's vital passion, of life itself. In the earlier portrait this blood has been dammed up by frustration or has flowed only after uncontrolled aggression; here the blood has been truly spilled, and the poet cannot bear the sight.

Let me not see it!	(¡Que no quiero verla!
Send word to the moon to come,	Dile a la luna que venga,
I cannot look upon the blood	que no quiero ver la sangre
Of Ignacio upon the sand.	de Ignacio sobre la arena.
Send warning to the jasmine flowers,	¡Avisad a los jazmines
With their tints of white!	con su blancura pequeña!

At this point in the poem Lorca utilizes one of the great symbols of mythology: "The cow of the ancient world/passed her sad

[112]

tongue/over the snouts of blood/spilled upon the sand." This symbolic cow, a bit later in the poem changed to the "terrible mothers," is a Jungian symbol of the Mother Earth, earth that always waits to take back its own. As is well known, the cow and moon symbols are associated together even in the mythology of Crete and ancient Egypt. What is impressive is the sense of reality Lorca achieves while using a symbol of the widest general meaning.

The poet now turns away from the sight of the blood to concentrate on the bullfighter's courage and presence. Ignacio in the unequal struggle against inevitable death has risen as high as courage could take anyone: "Up the grandstand ascends Ignacio,/death clinging to his back." In the moment of truth he passed the bull's horns close without flinching. When the poet begins the portrait of the living Ignacio, it is easy to imagine him, resplendent in his blue and gold "suit of lights."

There never was a Sevillian prince,	(No hubo príncipe en Sevilla
Who could with him compare;	que comparársele pueda,
Never a sword like his sword	ni espada como su espada
Nor even heart so true.	ni corazón tan de veras.
An air of Andalusian Rome	Aire de Roma andaluza
Shone golden round his face;	le doraba la cabeza
His laughter was a sparkling rose	donde su risa era un nardo
Of intelligence and grace.	de sal y de inteligencia.)

In Lorca's mind the Roman influence in Spain was always expressed through prudence, manliness and intelligence.

The poet follows with an apostrophe to the bullfighter which recalls immediately to the Spanish mind some of Jorge Manrique's famous lines praising his father:

What a grand bullfighter in the ring!	(¡Qué gran torero en la plaza!
In the mountains, mountaineer;	¡Qué gran serrano en la sierra!
How gentle with the heads of wheat,	¡Qué blando con las espigas!
How heavy with the spur!	¡Qué duro con las espuelas!
How tender with the falling dew,	¡Qué tierno con el rocío!

How brilliant in the fight;	¡Qué deslumbrante en la feria!
How tremendous with the final shafts,	¡Qué tremendo con las últimas
The banderillas of night!	banderillas de tiniebla!)

In the third section, "The Laid-out Body," the poet, becoming more restrained, is forcing himself to contemplate the body on the marble stone as he attempts to find "the way out/for this captain tied by death." The stanzas are in the formal Alexandrine, a balanced and noble verse. In the first stanzas, there is an elaboration of the stone as symbol. This stone is a "forehead where dreams weep," "a shoulder to carry time," a rock that shatters the waves. The stone ultimately receives all seed, all forms, bad or good; it gives only "bullrings and bullrings and bullrings without walls," that is, a repository of places of death. Thus Ignacio is now upon the stone, "rain gushes through his mouth," and "The air like a madman leaves his sunken chest." All around, "A silence heavy with stench reposes." Finally, the poet rouses himself to call upon those men who "break horses and tame rivers" to tell him the meaning of death. They have no answer; in fact, it is surprising that the poet should call upon the doers, who of course would be out taming rivers. Perhaps there is a loss of grasp at this point, for the imagery not only becomes of uncertain outline, but we also find a certain surly resignation. Indeed, Lorca says farewell with the soothing words, "Sleep, fly, repose," but his conclusion that "The sea will also die" is small consolation.

The final section, in fine hendecasyllables which sustain the elevated tone of the previous section, is entitled "Absent Spirit." In the first stanza, the poet stresses how quickly everyone has forgotten the dead; neither people nor horse nor even the ants remember him. Even memory of him has already vanished, because "he has died forever." Again Lorca suggests a smoldering rebellion in his imagery, for the bullfighter has vanished "like all the dead that are forgotten/in a pile of snuffed out dogs." But if all others forget, the poet will sing forever afterward his "profile and his grace," his knowledge and "The sadness found in his valiant joy." The concluding stanza has the eternal sadness characteristic of Lorca and suggests an epitaph for both bullfighter and poet:

Much time will pass before there appears again
An Andalusian so ardent for adventure.
I sing his elegance with words that moan,
And remember a breeze sad in the olive groves.

(Tardará mucho tiempo en nacer, si es que nace,
un andaluz tan claro, tan rico de aventura.
Yo canto su elegancia con palabras que gimen
y recuerdo una brisa triste por los olivos.)

Lorca's *Lament for the Death of a Bullfighter* is a moving poem, an honest expression of the poet's qualities and a significant expression of an important part of Spanish tradition. It is also a modern poem, for while it begins with great power, it tends to conclude in a whimper. Inevitably there springs a comparison with the noble elegy of Jorge Manrique, which moves grandly toward a climax in the final section. In an atmosphere of prayer, the father of Manrique's poem, surrounded by his family and loved ones, surrenders back his spirit to Him who gave it. Now the first three sections of Lorca's elegy are almost overwhelming, for Lorca is unsurpassed in presenting the existential position of man and his few hours of precious vitality under the inexorable shadow of death as nothingness. But the last section is pathetically (albeit honestly) entitled "Absent Spirit," because spirit is exactly what the poet could not infuse into the poem. Even as the poet sings to the memory of the bullfighter, he emphasizes presence, grace, appetite and elegance, all qualities which weakly suggest spirit. The poem therefore expresses the failure of modern man to find a spiritual meaning in life.

Lorca's *Lament* reveals his intuition in choosing the bullfighter as the figure which would most nobly express man's tragic existence at the expense of vitality. In this monument to Ignacio Sánchez Mejías, the bullfighter's courage and grace, his presence and performance become for Lorca values which must be sufficient unto themselves. Of course the creation of the poem itself, though Lorca never stressed it, bestows a limited immortality. Lorca's manipulation of various verse forms, the control of his extravagant metaphor and the orchestration of various parts into a structured poem indicate his poetic maturity. If we admit that Unamuno's *The Christ of Veláquez* is, while massive, a massive failure nevertheless, Lorca's *Lament for the Death of a Bullfighter* is perhaps the outstanding lyric poem in modern Spanish literature.

CHAPTER 6

Lorca and the Theater

I *Background of Lorca's Theater*

WHILE in the 1920's Lorca concentrated on poetry, in the early 1930's he decided to devote his basic energies to a renovation of the Spanish theater. Toward the end of his life, he was to declare with conviction: "The theater was always my vocation." In preparing himself for this vocation, Lorca not only attempted to assimilate the various currents in the European and Spanish drama, but he also worked directly with dramatic production. As we have seen, his early association with Martínez Sierra and the Eslava Theater had given him technical training. In his work with *La Barraca* he studied diligently and staged classical plays of Spain's seventeenth century; from them he wanted to preserve and modernize the enduring elements of his native Spanish tradition. At the same time, however, he was studying the successes of the playwrights of the vanguard, both in Spain and outside, and at the end he was moving toward the expression of the most modern themes, themes later to be exploited by the American Tennessee Williams and the French theater.

In his drama Lorca was undoubtedly sensitive to general European influences, although the limits are difficult to define.[1] Certainly his international success with the *Gypsy Ballads*, followed by his trip to America, had broadened his outlook. The emphases of Lorca's drama are those of European drama: the importance of the instincts; primitive drives, usually specifically sexual, overwhelming civilized reason; the problems of man's isolation; and death as enigma and finality. The theme of the individual struggle with the instincts is usually traced from Ibsen (*Peer Gynt*) through the Freudian period in the plays of the French dramatist Lenormand. Of course the "sexual problem" has become the touchstone of much modern drama, and as for man's isolation and alienation, Pirandello is the international name usually associated with it. In Spain, the major writers just prior to Lorca (most of whom tried drama) had assimilated these currents with varying emphases, and Lorca probably received much of his European influence through the Spanish writers.

When Lorca appeared on the literary scene, the Spanish theater was still dominated by Jacinto Benavente, winner of the Nobel Prize in 1922. Benavente's typical plays, comedies of urbane social satire, gradually became unsatisfactory to Lorca's generation. Benavente, however, was successful with many types of plays. His *The Passion Flower* (*La malquerida*), a rural drama of primitive drives, consciously or not for Lorca, became something of a model for his *Blood Wedding*. Benavente no doubt represented for him the successful playwright; from the beginning Lorca strove to write plays for a living theater.

Of primary influence on Lorca's drama was the tradition of what the Spanish critics have called the poetic theater in Spain. In this poetic theater, the outstanding representatives, such as Valle-Inclán, Jacinto Grau and the Machado brothers, attempted to continue the enduring elements of Spanish tradition while introducing some of the preoccupations of the modern world, in a literary form of high quality, but not necessarily poetry. Valle-Inclán, although immensely talented, like Unamuno soon lost faith in the commercial theater and began to produce a novelized dramatic work which was rarely seen on the stage. But in a series of powerful *Barbaric Comedies* (*Comedias bárbaras*), he showed the workings of the primitive instincts in tracing the psychological history of a family in Galicia. As his manner became increasingly macabre and grotesque, his work assumed a quality related to the Freudian-surrealist manner. His works such as *The Horns of Don Friolera* (*Los cuernos de don Friolera*) and *The Boy with the Silver Face* (*Cara de plata*) exerted an influence on Lorca which has not often been adequately emphasized.

Jacinto Grau and the Machados also wrote first-rate literary dramas not successful on the stage. Grau, returning to ancient myths and Spanish legend, attempted to create a work on two planes, the realistic and the illusory, at the same time. He achieved perhaps the most enduring play of this period on the Don Juan theme, *The Seducer Who Seduces Not* (*El burlador que no se burla*), in which Don Juan moves between reality and myth.

The Machado brothers, in addition to treating this same theme in their *Don Juan of Mañara,* attempted to modernize the poetic drama with specific details of Freudian psychology in *Bitter Oleander (Las adelfas),* but the play failed in the theater. It is a tribute to Lorca's talent that he had important success with poetic drama in the theater.

In approaching Lorca's drama, especially the minor works, we are fortunate to be able to utilize the dramatist's own analysis, made in a long interview in the last year of his life.[2] Lorca declares that for him the theater is "poetry that rises from the book and becomes human." But obviously the danger for the poet in becoming dramatist is that the former stresses individual preoccupations while the dramatist must achieve objective characterizations so as to provide conflict and structure. Lorca admits that "My first plays are unplayable," but then he goes on to add, "In these impossible plays is my true intention." He must mean that at least the "impossible plays" have too much of his personal emphasis, as we shall see clearly in *Mariana Pineda,* along with certain ambiguities in other plays. With these few words Lorca makes it unnecessary for the critic to seek desperately to explain the weaknesses of the minor plays,[3] and certain problems in the major ones. Of the "unplayable" group he mentions specifically *Thus Five Years Pass (Así que pasen cinco años).* He concludes that in order "to demonstrate a personality and earn respect" he continued to explore other types.

II *The Minor Dramatic Pieces*

Lorca's first mature effort in the drama is *Mariana Pineda,* begun perhaps as early as 1923. The play is based on an episode which occurred in Granada in the 1800's. In the play Mariana, a young widow with two children, is desperately in love with Don Pedro de Sotomayor, leader of a liberal uprising. The rebels appear in the house of Mariana, who is already uneasy because she is secretly embroidering a flag for the group. When Pedrosa, the leader of the conservative opposition, appears at the house, Don Pedro and the rebels flee, leaving Mariana to face the enemy. Pedrosa accuses her of embroidering the flag of rebellion, but promises her amnesty if she will denounce the rebels. At the same time he makes amatory advances. When Mariana rejects him completely, she is imprisoned in a convent. After a long period of isolation, she still refuses to denounce the rebels and is taken to the gallows.

This play, entirely in verse form, demonstrates Lorca's budding talent and his unwillingness at that time to develop a theme without undue personal preoccupations. Lorca, who first read the play to the Dalí family, indicated in 1927 that he had three distinct versions of it, the first ones "absolutely not feasible in the theater." He added that the final version had a double meaning that only a few would understand. The play is barely begun when there is a scene of puzzling and unnatural attraction between Mariana, a widow with children, and Amparo, a tomboyish young lady who wants to take her off to the bullfights. Amparo, whose speeches also reveal the author's enigmatic personal symbolism, says such things as "tremor of moon above a fishbowl/where silver fish pretends red dream." The middle act has some expected political direction, but the scenes reek of melodrama, as if the dramatist had suddenly lost either talent or interest. Then in the last act, as Mariana laments her hopeless fate, she seems to be headed inexorably toward the gallows, not because she loves liberty or loves Don Pedro (a shadowy figure clearly unworthy of her love), but merely because of love, which has never been a crime. In fact, all the agitation about "liberty" in the play has one meaning for the author, another for the audience. In short, the interaction between Mariana's tragically isolated love and the characters who are supposed to provide its strength is muddled and unconvincing, and the drama as a whole is in part a failure as a drama.

It is unfortunate that this should be so, for the play has at least two outstanding elements. First, Mariana is a convincing portrait of a woman tragically in love. Her lyric expression of this love is fine poetry, as when she first confesses: "For this true love/that devours my simple soul/I am becoming yellowed/like the rosemary flower." And at the end, Don Pedro having faded away, she laments as the hangman comes: "But I know well the meaning of that light!/Love, love, love, and eternal loneliness!" Throughout the play Mariana's love is tinged with foreboding, as if she were seeking martyrdom. The second outstanding feature of the play is its lyricism, especially in the three ballads. The first on the bullfights in Ronda is a sparkling poem in which the poet captures the·

movement and colors and excitement of the spectacle. Lorca had only limited success in working these poems into the dramatic action. It is in a sense unfortunate that he did not utilize these fine materials in a lyric work. Since at the simple level the words of love and the cry for liberty struck a responsive chord, *Mariana Pineda* has generally been treated benevolently by public and critics.

Around 1930, during the period of *Poet in New York*, Lorca experimented with various dramas and shorter pieces in the surrealist manner, with his own personal preoccupations as the center of his attention. As we have seen, these were critical years for Lorca, and he attempted to utilize his turbulence and confusion for artistic purpose. In 1928, he had written three pieces called *Brief Theater* (*Teatro breve*), with titles like "Buster Keaton's Walk" and "Chimera," sketches hardly worth the effort of deciphering. But *Thus Five Years Pass* (*Así que pasen cinco años*) is a full-length play, with a bewildering variety of scenes. The constant character is a Young Man, and into his world comes a Stenographer, a Lad, a Cat, a Rugby Player, a Mannequin, Card Players, etc. In Schonberg's fine analysis,[4] the basic conflict in the first act is between Love of the Young Man and Time, represented by the Old Man. The Stenographer, who is reality, is dismissed; thereby the Young Man can devote himself entirely to suspending his love in a dream state, the only protection against Time. The two Friends, in contrast, want to spend life, one in joys of the senses, the other in the artistic. Interposed in this action is a dream-sequence, a kind of nightmare, in which a Boy and his Cat pass rapidly through life into the void of nothingness.

In the second act the Young Man rejects the Fiancée of five years, who represents a kind of Death to him; she promptly runs off with a Rugby Player. The Young Man then has a dialogue with a Mannequin, perhaps a symbol of lost idealism, but finally decides to search out a new experience. In the last act Harlequin and a Clown joke together; then the scene shifts to a game of cards, where the young Man is forced to play his Ace of Hearts, his life card, Time and Death winning against Love. Thus ends this profound and complex experiment which bears the stamp of Lorca's intelligence. It is unfit for the stage, largely because of the density of themes and symbolism and lack of dramatic action.

In the same vein is an unfinished piece entitled *The Public* (*El Público*) (1930), of even more exaggerated symbolism and revolutionary idea.[5] In the "Roman Queen" section, a Vine Figure and a Bell Figure chatter symbolically while performing a kind of perverted sexual ballet, apparently for the benefit of the Emperor. The other section is a madhouse uprising of students and public at a performance of *Romeo and Juliet*, the main preoccupation being Juliet's real identity. Lorca's intent is apparently to insinuate a coming sexual revolution of absolute freedom. He had found this idea in Whitman.

Three of the minor dramatic pieces are clearly in the Spanish tradition, with Lorca's special thematic emphasis. *Love of Don Perlimplín with Belisa in the Garden* (*Amor de Don Perlimplín con Belisa en su jardín*), subtitled an "Erotic Halleluja," is a short farce which Lorca had plans to expand. In the play, Don Perlimplín, an aging bachelor, is persuaded to marry the lively young Belisa, whose mother encourages the match. Don Perlimplín is unable to consummate the marriage on the wedding night, and he is cuckolded by five shadowy lovers. Soon Belisa shamelessly confesses a young lover is pursuing her. Don Perlimplín offers to arrange a tryst for them in the garden. When the disguised lover appears, mortally wounded, it turns out to be Perlimplín himself, who has dreamed up the whole affair.

Lorca set out in Don Perlimplín to sustain an artistic balance between the lyric and the grotesque,[6] and, given a properly sensitive audience, the piece is a minor triumph. In Lorca's words, Don Perlimplín attempts to "cuckold all the women who exist," to create from his impotence an artistic plan so beautiful that Belisa's sensuality will be transformed into spirit. The audience is carried along in suspension between the near bawdy and the near angelic. Perhaps Belisa suffers from Lorca's persistent deprecation of the feminine as sensuality, but Don Perlimplín even with his golden horns evokes a mixture of pity and admiration. Don Perlimplín's triumph, which is also the author's, leaves in the audience a bittersweet reaction, perplexed between laughter and tears, but deeply moved.

From what was probably a more extensive collection, two of Lorca's pantomimes (or puppet shows) have survived, the *Pantomime of Don Christopher* (*Retablillo de Don Cristóbal*) and the

Puppet Show of the Cachiporra (*Los títeres de Cachiporra*), in which many of the elements of *Don Christopher* are repeated, with many new characters and comic scenes. From an early age Lorca was attracted to the puppet show as it was presented in Spain, and as he matured apparently he adopted it to express his mixture of irony, innocence, laughter and social criticism. In the *Pantomime of Don Christopher*, he has the poet in a prologue warn the presumably cultured audience that the puppets will use the joyful, simple and innocent expressions of the country. Now of course Lorca did not really believe the ridiculous idea that peasant vulgarity is more innocent than any other; this is a way safely to attack bourgeois prejudices. Don Christopher, the typical old lecher of tradition, comes upon the Little Rosa's mother, who promptly sells her daughter for an ounce of gold. When Little Rosa appears, her aims are clear. In a kind of burlesque of a famous speech of Don Juan, Little Rosa says she wants to play, "on the divan with Juan, in the canapé with José, on the floor with him I adore, etc." Little Rosa's utterances begin thus and get worse—it is excellent humor of a bawdy sort. When Don Christopher and Rosa are finally together, the former proves to be impotent and drops off to sleep; when he awakens, Rosa, who has cuckolded him during his sleep, is giving birth to quadruplets. In the usual confusion at the end of the puppet show, Don Christopher is beating everyone in sight with his club. In this exaggeration of a popular tradition, Lorca's scatological imagery, sparkling dialogue and rapid movement are overwhelming; again he has used his artistic talent to prick cultural pretensions, with no one sure where innocence ends and vicious irony begins.

CHAPTER 7

Five Major Dramas

I The Shoemaker's Prodigious Wife
(La zapatera prodigiosa)

IN the study of Lorca's drama, the farce of *The Shoemaker's Prodigious Wife* is of decisive importance. Written at a time when he was poised between tradition and vanguard, the work demonstrates his ability to utilize the basic Spanish materials successfully, while working toward an introduction of some of the newer ideas. He tells us that he conceived and wrote the first version of the farce in 1926, during a visit to his home in Granada. Having left the world of Madrid and Barcelona where agitation over the vanguard movement raged, he experienced again the attraction of the simple and timeless in provincial Andalusia. This "fable with direct reality" was staged in the *Teatro Español* in Madrid in 1930. Lorca continued to revise the original version, apparently toward greater abstraction, and the newer version was staged in Buenos Aires in 1933.

As the play begins, the author as a character appears on the stage and speaks directly to his audience, invoking it to use poetic imagination in reacting to the work. He asks not for benevolence but for attention. At this point the Shoemaker's Wife threatens to burst upon the stage before time, and the author, as if overwhelmed by the vitality of his created character, timidly retires. The Wife, ready for passionate argument, takes the stage and is soon in bitter dialogue with her husband the Shoemaker. The pretty and exuberant young wife forms a striking contrast with the diligent but unassertive Shoemaker, a man about fifty years old.

The young Wife wants excitement, romance, action, but the poor Shoemaker wants to stay at his cobbler's bench with peace and quiet. When the Mayor appears, the Shoemaker desperately asks his advice in his marital dilemma. The Mayor counsels for the woman a strong hug, a voice at shouting pitch and, if all else fails, the club of authority. Others enter the shop, the men to flirt with the Wife, the women to haggle with the Shoemaker over prices. The Shoemaker becomes more and more upset over not being able to control his wife, and he finally decides to disappear. The Wife receives the news from her friend, a Little Boy on whom she lavishes her maternal affection. As the first act ends with the neighbor women gathered around, the Shoemaker's Wife is tearfully lamenting being left alone.

As the second act begins, the Wife is running the tavern she has established. To it come the men of the town, the younger ones to pay her court, the oldsters like Don Blackbird bearing dishonest intentions. The Wife, however, rejects them with abuse or with humor, proclaiming her loyalty to her husband. Soon the sounds of music herald the arrival of a puppeteer at the tavern door, and all gather to see his show. The Puppeteer is the Shoemaker in disguise, and although his repertoire is large, including tales of highwaymen and classical heroes, he chooses to begin for the townspeople "The Deeds of the Too-meek Shoemaker." In fine ballad form the disguised Shoemaker recites the story of himself and his wife, and this moves the Wife to tears. But the ending given the ballad by the Shoemaker describes how the Wife and a Suitor are making plans to kill the Shoemaker.

At this moment, someone shouts that two young men are in a knife fight over the Shoemaker's Wife. As everyone rushes away, the Shoemaker and the Wife have an opportunity to declare their love for each other, still without recognition. The formerly meek Shoemaker finally receives a full declaration of submission from the Wife. This gained, he reveals his identity. At the conclusion, the Wife is again scourging the neighbors and lamenting her fate, but she is doing it happily, secure in the knowledge that the two of them will hereafter defend their home.

The Shoemaker's Prodigious Wife is Lorca's first satisfying dramatic work, within the limitations, as some see them, of the farce as a major form. Lorca has stylized in the structure of a ballet or operetta a traditional Andalusian theme. Obviously, the work is related to de Falla's *The Three-Cornered Hat* (*El sombrero de tres picos*), which he had adapted from a short novel. Lorca was associated with the Theater Eslava group at the time de Falla's ballet was staged, and he had a continuing interest in blending the arts of music, painting and poetry. Certain characters in Lorca's *The Shoemaker's Prodigious Wife*—the neighbor women for example —are handled mainly as figures of movement and color. Music is used to heighten the comic effects, as when Don Blackbird is introduced with an exaggerated polka.

Lorca's blending of dialogue, poetry and song is also very effective.[1] In the dialogue, which is usually prose, he was attempting to capture the rhythms of Andalusian speech. The speech of the Wife is particularly expressive, ranging from the exuberant abuse she flings at the neighbors to the tender expressions used with the Boy. The exchanges are brisk and sparkling, the utterances racy and natural, with almost no tendency toward an enigmatic symbolism. The Shoemaker's Wife introduces various popular songs, created by Lorca himself, but fitting into the context of the drama. When the Little Boy recites a poem as he unsuccessfully chases a butterfly, Lorca uses the tender mood created to achieve strong contrast, for the Boy has come to tell his friend that the Shoemaker has deserted her. When the disguised Shoemaker recites the long ballad, their own story thinly concealed, the ballad is central to the play, and worked properly into the action. Lorca's achievement is to have created all these stylized elements, then to blend them into a total effect which seems natural and imaginatively logical.

The dramatist's outstanding achievement in the play is the creation of the character of the Shoemaker's Wife. The role was first perfected by the great actress Margarita Xirgu, and other outstanding actresses attempted it later. The Shoemaker's Wife is a type of character in an ancient Spanish tradition dating back to the period of the old ballads. Menéndez Pidal has shown that in the Spanish ballads of the theme of the unhappily married wife, the Spanish woman typically rejects the insistent suitor, however unhappy her condition. Following this tradition, Lorca properly uses the secondary characters to accentuate the many facets of her personality. In her friendship with the Little Boy she reveals the deep and tender maternal instinct. With the young suitors she shows fire, sparkle and romantic inclinations, controlled by wit and a sense of propriety. With the lascivious old suitor she displays a sense of reality and an ability to protect her personal worth. Against the aggressive neighbor women she defends fiercely the value of her husband's labor. In the character of the Shoemaker, Lorca wisely creates a figure who, if under the shadow of impotence and timidity, nevertheless ultimately discovers the strength of will to keep the Wife in the place she by her nature really prefers. The Shoemaker's Wife at the end is properly directing her energy and strength to the security of the home.

It is interesting to see how Lorca gradually came to insist upon the abstract elements of the play. In 1933, in a newspaper article for the Buenos Aires opening, he called it "the myth of our pure illusion unsatisfied." [2] Thus Lorca attempts to deny the reality in the farce, and to stress the music and rhythm and poetry. He has the Shoemaker's Wife respond to her surroundings as if in a dream, "the horseshoes of the suitor's horse,/Four sighs of silver." Obviously here is the intrusion of Lorca's bitter isolation, the world of Mariana Pineda and the theme of much of his poetry. But the audience will continue to respond to this farce as an achievement in reality, expertly touched with poetic imagination.

II Doña Rosita the Spinster (Doña Rosita la soltera)

The play *Doña Rosita the Spinster*, subtitled "Language of the Flowers," was germinating a long time in Lorca's mind. Lorca conceived a type of Andalusian woman like Doña Rosita in a poem around 1920. Then in 1924, as Lorca recalled later, Moreno Villa told him a story about a new *rosa mutabile,* a rose red in the morning, white in the afternoon, and already losing its leaves at nightfall. The symbolic values of such a rose struck Lorca immediately, and it became the leitmotif of *Doña Rosita*. Lorca later told Margarita Xirgu a fanciful tale of finding in the attic an old book on horticulture which described the *rosa mutabile*. Both versions are poetically true. In any case, it was December, 1935, when the play was finally staged in Barcelona, with Margarita Xirgu in the main role. Although the performance was a triumph, the play was attacked as being political because of certain speeches in it against the rich, and it never reached Madrid.

In implementation of the three stages of the *rosa mutabile,* Lorca constructed the three acts of the drama to represent three distinct epochs in Doña Rosita's life. The first, set in the year 1885 when Rosita was twenty, was during the time of hoopskirts, complicated hairdos, parasols. The second, of 1900, was a time of the cinched waist, the Exposition of Paris, the first automobiles. The final act takes place in 1911, with another change of fashions, with the airplane, the threat of world war. In the three acts Lorca attempts to capture the changes in Doña Rosita, her family and her world.

In the first act, Rosita, a young girl orphaned early, is living with her aunt and uncle, the latter a horticulturist preoccupied with the development of new rose types, especially the *rosa mutabile*. The Aunt lives in a perpetual discussion with the Housekeeper, a devoted soul but a chronic complainer. Rosita, a charming, quiet girl, is happily in love with her young cousin. Three young ladies come to visit, voicing their quietly desperate hope and illusion of finding love in Granada. Suddenly the cousin decides he must go to South America where his father needs him, but he promises to return to marry Rosita.

At the beginning of the second act, fifteen years have passed, and a shadow of industry has reached Granada. The industrialist who chats with the Uncle could be a suitor for Rosita, but she is still waiting for the Cousin. Life in the house goes on monotonously. The Housekeeper is becoming more querulous, is more worried for Doña Rosita. Rosita stays close to the house, because in the street she is too conscious of how time is passing and she "does not want to lose her illusions." Three spinsters come to visit, and chat emptily and endlessly. Doña Rosita is becoming a quiet shadow, a worry for the whole household. Finally a letter comes from America, but the Cousin suggests vaguely a marriage by proxy, and promises that he will come later. Although the Housekeeper is skeptical, Rosita is still grasping at this pitiful hope as the act ends.

At the beginning of the third act, eleven years more have passed, and reality has come crushingly down. The Uncle has died, and the women are being forced to move to a more modest house. A poor professor drops by the home with a long and discouraging story of his teaching situation. He is filled with knowledge, an abstract knowledge of harmony and rhetoric and poetry to be sure, but his students are unconcerned brutes, their parents interested only in material gains. An honest letter finally comes from America; the Cousin has been married for eight years. And Doña Rosita, who has hoped and suffered and endured, at last begins to find her voice. In the last part of the act she struggles to define her suffering and loneliness, but she can only conclude by repeating the fate of the *rosa mutabile*: "When night comes slowly down/It begins to shed its leaves."

In *Doña Rosita the Spinster* Lorca was attempting to blend the poetic with a picture of the customs and manners of Andalusia in the past.[3] The poetic of course deals largely with the illusory; the customs and manners are more realistic. In Doña Rosita with her unwavering hope lies what is poetic; in the other characters is the stifling and petty reality. Lorca's intention was deftly ironic in presenting his picture of the pettiness of the Granadine culture. As usual his male characters are ineffective beings with only a limited will. The continued arguments between the Aunt and the Housekeeper, with the Uncle at times included, are intended to be a truthful presentation of domestic life. But in order to point up this irony, the long scenes of directionless existence keep Lorca in constant danger of making the whole play boring.

What saves *Doña Rosita the Spinster* is the fine balance of the poetic materials. Although the dialogue is usually in prose, early in the play the Uncle recites the poem of the *rosa mutabile*, which he has actually grown. Until noon the rose is "red like blood," but in the late afternoon it turns white, and after the fall of night it begins to lose its leaves. The appropriate section of the delicate poem is repeated in each act throughout the play. Lorca also cast the difficult scene of the Cousin's proposal and his promise to return in poetic form. Although we know from the very title that the promise is not to be fulfilled, at the moment Rosita and the young man convince us with no hint of irony. In this same act, Rosita presents in a moving ballad the plight of all the romantic lasses of Granada, "Those who go down to the Alhambra/By threes and by fours, alone." In implementation of the sub-title of the play, the ladies in the parlor recite the "language of the flowers," that is, the particular sentiment suggested by each flower. This language of the flowers suggests a tradition utilized by the dramatists of the Golden Age. The poetic but tragic Granada which emerges from the play is Lorca's typical view.

As a character, Doña Rosita is perhaps more a symbol than a person, since she is not developed psychologically. What she has is *presence*, the suggestion of a great well of profundity without exact contours. Lorca had conceived Doña Rosita as a type as early as his *Book of Poems*, around 1920. At the beginning she is that promise of vitality and gayety which abide. Through the first acts she speaks importantly only in the scene of the engagement. But we see the effect of her presence in the whole family, who show their love for her and their desperate uneasiness and compassion as her beauty and her hope begin to fade. Since Lorca saw Doña Rosita as "meek on the outside and full of fire within," it is only natural that she should burst her shell and attempt to speak at the end of the play. Doña Rosita says that if the people had not reminded her so constantly of her spinsterhood, she could have sustained her illusion to the end, could have lived contentedly on hope. But now she is suffering the worst of all feelings, the realization that hope is dead. All that is left her is dignity, and her determination not to be bitter and hateful. Doña Rosita is thus another example of Lorca's theme of the frustrated woman, this time both physically and spiritually. Of all the characters of his drama, Lorca himself preferred Doña Rosita, for she was to him a symbol of Granada and solitude and lost youth.

Lorca's achievement in *Doña Rosita the Spinster* lies basically in the evocation of a decayed past, with perhaps some indication of a struggle toward change. As critics have pointed out, certainly the last scene of *Doña Rosita* recalls the atmosphere of the final scene of Chekhov's *The Cherry Orchard*. Moreover, Lorca's use of a natural symbol, the rose, to suggest the decay makes us suspect that Lorca was aware of Chekhov's play with its symbol of the cherry orchard. Doña Rosita briefly seems to become conscious of her situation as a problem to be attacked, but her creator, himself an Andalusian "static and tragic," allows her in her final speech to retreat into poetry, to become the rose whose leaves are beginning to fall.

III   Blood Wedding (Bodas de Sangre)

Lorca's most enduringly popular drama, both in the Hispanic countries and internationally, has been *Blood Wedding*. Many would call it the best of all his plays. The premiere performance in Madrid in March, 1933, was an outstanding success, as was a second premiere by a different company in Buenos Aires in 1933. While the initial performance in English translation in New York in 1935 received adverse judgments from the critics, the drama has since become a standard item even in the United States, especially in university theater. It has also been popular in France and even in Russia. Certainly *Blood Wedding* was very close to Lorca; it is almost a complete summary of his poetic and dramatic practices. But this closeness tends to make it a "problem" play, with one level of meaning for Lorca, another for the public—the same situation as in *Mariana Pineda*. Lorca himself was uneasy before the premiere, not about how the play would be received, but about how it would be interpreted. It is significant that a usually benevolent critic like Valbuena Prat has been very unenthusiastic toward *Blood Wedding*. But the work surely has a certain stamp of genius and deserves close study.

The basic action takes place in a rural area of Andalusia, as in *Yerma*. The characters and situation are introduced in the three scenes of the first act. The Mother, who has lost her husband and other sons in a blood feud, is discussing the wedding plans of the surviving son, the Bridegroom. He is to marry a girl who lives on a farm some distance away. The mother is bitterly displeased that the Bride-to-be was once the sweetheart of Leonardo, of the Félix family, the same family which had killed her loved ones. In the second scene in Leonardo's house the situation is ominous. Although Leonardo married another girl and now has a child, he has been ignoring the family and storming about the countryside on a horse. The news of the coming wedding stirs consternation in his family. In the third scene, Mother and Bridegroom visit the house of the Bride. In this scene she is a quiet, respectful girl who helps to arrange the details of the marriage that will consolidate the property of the two families.

The second act begins with the bustle of preparations for the wedding. The Bride is beginning to show reluctance, and the appearance of Leonardo adds to the turbulence. Soon the young people of the village arrive and begin to sing and recite lovely wedding songs for the Bride. This scene continues for many minutes, the young people animated and joyful, the elders joyfully melancholy. Scene two begins with the return of the company from wedding ceremony. There is a great bustling about, with drinking and dancing. The Bride shows herself reluctant to accept the Groom's caresses. Leonardo and his horse have disappeared, but suddenly there is a report that Leonardo and the Bride have fled on the horse. The act ends in confusion, with the Mother screaming for a horse so that the Groom can set out in pursuit.

The last act, largely written in verse, begins in a wood, where a group of stylized Woodcutters are discussing the ominous events. Suddenly two symbolic figures appear, an old Beggarwoman representing Death and a Young Woodcutter, the Moon; both figures are meant to represent the overwhelming instincts of the lovers. The furious Bridegroom appears, searching for the pair. In a heavily sensual scene, Leonardo and the Bride discuss their mutual attraction and their fate. They go offstage and shrieks are heard. The old Beggarwoman appears as Death and silently shows her dominance as the scene ends. In the following scene someone passes the word that the young men are bringing the bodies of Leonardo and the Bridegroom back to the village. As the play ends, the grieving Mother and the Bride, both sunk in hate, are nevertheless joined together by the eternal tragedy which has no remedy.

In *Blood Wedding*, there is, parallel to the basic action at the realistic level, an extensive development of theme and sub-theme at the symbolical level. The theme of the fruits of the land is introduced as the Bridegroom takes the knife to go out to cut a bunch of grapes. This simple act allows the Mother to approach the theme of the knife as destructive. The leitmotif of the Knife as a death symbol persists to the end of the play. In the dialogue that follows, she proceeds to reveal herself as overprotective of the Bridegroom, and little by little he shows himself willing to be overprotected. From the first act Lorca begins to suggest that the Bridegroom is reluctant.

In an early scene Lorca introduces the symbol of the horse as another leitmotif, the horse at the simplest level serving as the symbol of the sexual instincts. Even before we hear of Leonardo's thundering around the Bride's house on his horse, Lorca presents the motif in an extended cradle song. Around the cradle of Leonardo's child, the Mother-in-law hums what on the surface seems to be an innocent lullaby, but the song is about a horse, a big horse, which "wanted not the water." Moreover, this horse has "wounded hooves and frozen mane." Since these images suggest impotence, from this point there is something enigmatic in the work, for the horse is clearly associated with Leonardo, whose instincts seem to be over-powering.

In the second act Lorca creates an atmosphere of joy and expectation with the elaborate variations of popular wedding songs: "Let the bride awaken/On her wedding morn. Let rivers of earth/Bear her shining crown!" The servant, the bridesmaids, even the young men join in this tribute of deep social significance. While Lorca's songs are original, they evoke immediately the living tradition of some of Lope de Vega's dramas, especially *Peribáñez*. But the critics have failed to stress the fact that Lorca creates his beautiful scene for a harshly ironic purpose, since hard on the heels of it comes the shocking news that the Bride has fled with Leonardo. It is surprising that this abduction scene closely resembles a like one in Ibsen's *Peer Gynt,* as de la Guardia has pointed out.[4]

The penultimate scene in the humid wood was undoubtedly a triumph for Lorca, because whatever confusion it shows was probably deliberate on his part. That the scene is powerful no one can deny. The unrealistic tone is a distinct shift from that of the earlier acts. Very soon comes the presentation of the struggle between the Beggarwoman and the Moon symbol for the life of the lovers or of the pursuing Bridegroom. The old Beggar-woman represents Death, but here the Moon symbol is associated with the sexual, an expansion of the earlier horse symbol. The fact that the Moon is a young man is clearly suggestive of further enigma, perhaps of a sexual nature. When next the scene of great sensuality occurs between Leonardo and the Bride, from the moment the Bride utters "What unreason!" the dialogue reveals ambiguity. Admittedly, thousands of playgoers have accepted this scene, but to one who understands Lorca's preferred imagery, the insinuation of homosexual imagery is unmistakable.

Two further moments in the play are important. It is significant that the men of the village come bringing the dead "lovers" (Leonardo and the Bridegroom) together from the wood, "Dark the one, dark the other," while a chorus chants, "Upon the golden flower, dirty sand." Moreover, in spite of the savage sensuality expressed by the Bride and the compromising situation in which she found herself, later she insists that she is "untouched, that no man has looked on her." A critic has developed the thesis that this play is on the honor theme of the Golden Age and therefore entirely within the Spanish tradition, but we find his argument unconvincing.[5]

The substance of *Blood Wedding* is Lorca's recurring theme of the overpowering instincts, the primordial passions which are hedged about by convention until they become aggressive, with death the only logical solution; and what is impressive is how much of himself Lorca is able to include in the tragedy, of his predilections, his past work and tradition. The theme of repressed vital passion is that of the *Poem of the Cante Jondo*, the *Gypsy Ballads* and *Poet in New York*, all with a differing emphasis. The symbols are the same symbols. From Spanish comedy comes the rural atmosphere. The death symbolism suggests Antonio Machado and Valle-Inclán, with more remote suggestion from European sources. The atmosphere of the wedding is remotely from Lope de Vega, but with altered purpose. The attempt to fuse the poetic and the realistic Lorca also tried in *Yerma*, but now with total success.

The only convincing character in *Blood Wedding* is the Mother. It is significant that a leading Spanish actress chose this role over that of the Bride, for the Mother has a consistency throughout the play. In the beginning she is the too-dominant influence on the son. She is the strength that holds the family together, the realistic force that provides for the continuity of life, tragic though it may be. She is the first to call for a horse to pursue the lovers who have shattered her family's honor. And she is the tragic figure who waits until the body of her beloved son is returned to her. She will weep, she will rail out at the dangerous games of men, but she will endure. With reason she has been compared in some ways to the woman in Synge's *Riders to the Sea*. The Mother was the one character Lorca could create with profound simplicity.

A modern drama of outstanding impact, *Blood Wedding* is successful, in part because the theater audience has accepted it enthusiastically, but mainly because in it Lorca achieved what he set out to do. The very title of the play may well have involved his profound questioning of the union of man and woman. We suggest that in *Blood Wedding*, as he had in *Don Perlimplín* and *Mariana Pineda*, he planned to write a work on two levels, with one meaning for the audience and another for himself. In other words, Lorca used his artistic talent to create a work the audience would judge traditional while he knew that at the same time he was subtly attacking the traditional social system. We are not trying to deny his right to do this; the modern artist seems often at cross-purposes with his audience. In *Blood Wedding* the interplay of the poetic and the realistic, the sincere and the ironic, the lucid and the enigmatic indicates that Lorca had not yet come to terms with himself or with his culture.

IV Yerma

Of all Lorca's plays, *Yerma* and *Blood Wedding* were the two which established his definitive reputation as a playwright. *Yerma*, first presented in December, 1934, at the Teatro Español in Madrid, had a run of more than a hundred performances. Apparently he had written a first version of the drama in New York around 1930, but the one finally staged must have been considerably reworked. Since *Yerma* (the title and also the female protagonist of the play) is in Spanish the adjective form of *yermo*, which means "barren land," there is a suggestion of Eliot's *The Waste Land*. Certainly it could have been written during the period of *Poet in New York*, which has specific echoes of Eliot. The theme of Lorca's *Yerma* indicates even more clearly, however, spiritual kinship with Unamuno, who in his desperate hunger for a life after death, explored the maternal instinct as a kind of symbol of the desire for immortality.

As *Yerma* begins, the audience hears a stylized cradle song which introduces the theme. Yerma has been married for two years to Juan, a farmer of ample means, and she is still awaiting a child. Juan, interested almost exclusively in his fields and land, feels little urge toward fatherhood. When her friend María, an expectant Mother, passes by, Yerma is anxious to question her about the pain and great joy of motherhood. Then when Victor, a young farmer, comes to the house, Yerma feels instinctively an attraction to him as a man who could fulfill her maternal ambitions, but even more strongly she feels bound by honor to be faithful to Juan. In talking to an Old Woman, Yerma first conceives the notion of using magic to help achieve maternity.

The second act begins with a stylized chorus of Washer-women, who alternate between gossip and song, all of it bearing on Yerma and her plight: "Woe unto the barren wife!" When the scene changes, Juan, now suspicious of Yerma's conduct, has brought his unmarried sisters into the house to watch her. The relation between Yerma and Juan is becoming more strained. Victor returns to the house, but only to say good-bye; his leaving is obviously an honorable way of separating himself from Yerma.

In the beginning of the third act Yerma, still determined to seek supernatural help toward maternity, is returning at dawn from a session in the cemetery with the Old Woman. Before she reaches home, Juan discovers her, and during the scene she is almost in a hysterical state. The second scene repeats Yerma's quest in an elaborate symbolic fashion. This stylized mountain scene, written in verse form, seems to be a mixture of Greek chorus, pagan fertility rite and religious pilgrimage. Again Yerma cries out for a child, but when the *Macho,* the symbol of male fertility, appears she refuses, invoking her bond of honor to her husband. As Yerma comes back to reality, with Juan still woodenly refusing to desire a child, she suddenly seizes him and chokes him to death, screaming, "I myself have killed my son!"

Without doubt *Yerma* is one of the most ambitious of Lorca's dramas. The tragedy follows an emphatic and unwavering line to the forceful conclusion. The theme is generally developed at two levels. First the theme is unfolded as the simple characters interact in their normal environment. Then, in alternating scenes, the theme is elaborated in stylized fashion, with songs, choruses and the important hermitage scene in the mountains somewhat in the fashion of Greek tragedy. Lorca was thus striving to provide a convincing example of the poetic theater which his generation admired but which few of them actually produced.

Perhaps the most outstanding weakness of the drama is the characterization of Juan and his relation to Yerma. Lorca's attitude toward normal manhood made it difficult for him to create male characters who were not ineffective or even burlesqued. Apparently he did not intend for Juan to be sterile, although Dr. Valbuena has suggested that the play should actually be named *Yermo,* since Juan is the barren one.[6] If Juan were sterile, then Yerma could only feel pity, and there would be no dramatic conflict. But Juan, who in every other way seems a sober, decisive individual, makes such clumsy protestations in avoiding love and desire for a child that we could easily suspect Lorca of irony. Yerma blames Juan for not giving her a child, and we are supposed to pity her because her deepest yearnings are unfulfilled. Yet we find ourselves pitying Juan instead, since he seems to be masking problems as profound as Yerma's. As the work stands, Yerma's final gripping scene is indeed a tragic necessity for her, but too much of our sympathy remains with Juan.

We also find another weakness in the play. Lorca insisted on using simple country people as characters, because he generally thought the bourgeois class (to which he actually belonged) to be effete and hypocritical. Now the naturalistic kind of author could depict even unlettered people convincingly, because he had them acting largely by instinct. Somehow Lorca strains our credulity by having his characters argue subtly, speak in elaborate symbol, then shift to a comment on stabling the oxen. Moreover, his female characters have a persistent tendency to speak symbolically, especially on sexual matters. This can be tolerated in stylized material such as songs, but it smacks of being merely incorrect in normal dialogue. He was much more successful with the dialogue in *The Shoemaker's Prodigious Wife.*

Even with these faults, *Yerma* is a fine play. It has appealed especially to Spanish audiences, probably because it deals with two enduring Spanish themes: the strength of the maternal instinct and the theme of honor. The final scene brings together the various symbolic elements of the play, among them, the Old Woman as Sorceress, the idea of a pilgrimage and the pagan fertility rites. Perhaps Lorca intended the scene as a dream projection by Yerma, with the Old Woman in contact with the forces that govern the fertility rites. Surely these rites represent the natural instincts; the pilgrimage represents civilized morality. And when Yerma chooses to retain the bond of honor to her husband, she is choosing Christian and Spanish morality. She can murder by instinct, but she cannot violate the bond of honor even to fulfill the maternal instinct. Perhaps the play is not a great tragedy, as Angel del Río has concluded. Lorca is strong in handling the poetic symbol and the effective plastic scene, but in the psychological penetration of characters, the ability to conceive a consistent base for his theme and the sustaining of a unified tone in his abstract scenes he was still learning.[7] But as an experiment in tragedy, *Yerma* is no mean achievement.

V   The House of Bernarda Alba
(La casa de Bernarda Alba)

In June, 1936, just two months before his death, Lorca read this drama before a small group in the house of the Count of Yepes. After Lorca's death the manuscript remained with his family, and it was not until 1945 that Margarita Xirgu finally staged the work in Buenos Aires. The Spanish premiere followed in 1950. In this drama, Lorca indicates a change from his former position of defending poetry in the drama. Since apparently he must have been criticized for using poems or songs in his earlier plays to cloak a lack of dramatic interaction, in *The House of Bernarda Alba* he used a dialogue of severe simplicity, with "not a drop of poetry." As in the case of *Blood Wedding*, the plot has been traced to a real episode in Andalusia during Lorca's youth; but of course his imagination and peculiar outlook on life made it impossible for him to be no more than a reporter. In this drama, then, Lorca is attempting with some objectivity to depict the deeper realities of Spanish life.

At the beginning of the play, Bernarda and her five daughters have just returned from the funeral of their father, accompanied by a group of ladies in mourning. With Bernarda, the ladies chant a kind of litany for the departed husband. Soon Bernarda has expressed strong anti-masculine sentiments; of course a neighbor mutters that she is really "pining for the heat of a male." When the mourners depart, Bernarda flails their hypocrisy and begins to demonstrate the cruel and inflexible authority that she wields in the house. First she heavy-handedly puts the servants in their places; then she proceeds to ride roughshod over the wills of the girls. But from Angustias, who is thirty-nine, to Adela, who is twenty, there is an undercurrent of fury and rebellion which increases throughout the play. As a group the girls are unresigned to the mother's dictum that they will remain in mourning for eight years, isolated from male companionship. In this atmosphere lives also Bernarda's ancient mother, a poor, demented thing who represents what all these females will become. With what mental faculties she has left, she prattles of wanting to discover "a beautiful male to marry, to find happiness with."

The one available male is Pepe the Roman. He is engaged to Angustias, but wants her only for her dowry. Soon Angustias is making plans for a wedding, and the atmosphere of hatred in the household becomes intensified. The servant finds out that Pepe is playing the double game of courting Angustias early at night, then returning to see an eager Adela later. Adela, confronted by the maid, refuses to desist, and when the maid tells Bernarda, she refuses to believe that anyone would defy her authority. When one of the girls steals Angustias' picture of Pepe, the state of rebellion and recrimination approaches a climax. At the end of the second act, the news spreads rapidly that a poor single girl of the village has had an illegitimate child, has killed and hid it among the stones, but the dogs have found the body. Now the people are stoning the poor girl. Bernarda cries out for the girl's death, while poor Adela trembles in foreboding.

In the third act, the repressed passion and hatred break out into open rebellion. It becomes clear that Adela has been slipping out of the house to see Pepe, but when Bernarda accosts her Adela grabs her cane and breaks the symbol of authority. Adela even feels that Pepe the Roman will come and "dominate this whole house." Her authority thus threatened on two fronts, Bernarda runs for a gun and fires it at Pepe; in the confusion which follows someone tells Adela that Pepe has been killed, though in fact he has escaped. Adela then goes to her room and hangs herself. As the play ends Bernarda is trying to re-assert her authority, insisting that the world will know that Adela "has died a virgin," and that once alone the family will drown themselves in a "sea of mourning."

The House of Bernarda Alba depends largely on the character of Bernarda and on the daughters whom she strives to control. Bernarda is something of a monster, a titanic figure all of a piece. Within a limited dimension she is convincing and heroic as the proponent of a system; she defends her concept of honor and responsibility with a fierceness which approaches mania. As a role, Bernarda has been a challenge to actresses. But she is a crystallized figure of rigid authority from the beginning; she shows no development of character at all. The daughters are even more rigid—Adela, for example, revealing an erotic fixation amounting to a mania. This group of near-hysterical women crash in mutual and violent conflict, enduring in a turbulent but meaningless tragedy with no solution possible. Such a conclusion does not indicate faking on the dramatist's part; Lorca himself, with his usual duality, was still tending to see life as an arena in which those who love merely torture each other, where friendship hardly exists and where the only value is struggle itself.

In writing *The House of Bernarda Alba* Lorca was beginning to experiment with social realism. It is well known that from the time of his visit to New York, Lorca was drawn to the movement toward social upheaval of the 1930's. This developing social consciousness and the awareness of his literary stature surely turned him toward meaningful social criticism of Spain. The great figures of the 20th century, such as Unamuno, Pío Baroja, Pérez de Ayala and even a poet like Antonio Machado, had preceded him in taking a hard look at the hypocrisy which suffused social customs, especially the relations between the sexes. In his play, Lorca portrays Bernarda as feeling herself in an embattled position, protecting her family against the enemy. But why should Pepe and the scarce suitors be such aliens, interested only in material gains? Why should the whole family be imprisoned by the envy and ill-will which surrounded them? Lorca as yet provides us no answers, but his growing concern with the poor indicates that he was beginning to question the inequalities of the social system itself. Bernarda is extremely callous with her faithful servants of long standing, insisting that they are "like animals, made of another substance." In the last year of his life, Lorca remarked that he was thinking in terms of "pure socialism." [8]

Final critical judgment on *The House of Bernarda Alba* as drama has been difficult. Perhaps the play indicates that Lorca the poet was finally accepting the challenge of drama that, although poetic from within, has no external dependence on music and poetic form. Certainly *Bernarda Alba* is technically well-constructed. The tragic theme, suggested by the appearance of the women in mourning in the first scene, is sustained throughout the play, properly reaching its greatest intensity at the climax. Roberto Sánchez, who thinks the play has the "somber and threatening" atmosphere of Castile and not Andalusia, is able to conclude that it is the culminating point of Lorca's drama.[9] We believe that *Blood Wedding* more adequately represents the sum of Lorca's talents and thematic preference as playwright. *The House of Bernarda Alba*, like all of his plays, was an example of his continuing experimentation. Unfortunately his death came when apparently he was just reaching maturity as a dramatist.

VI *Conclusions on Lorca's Drama*

García Lorca's permanent position among the dramatists of his generation and in Spanish literature in general has not yet been established, since he is still considered as a figure both historical and contemporary. His only competition for the position of the leading dramatist of the Generation of 1927 has been Alejandro Casona, whose work was overshadowed by Lorca's in the 1930's. Casona, whose successful career spanned the years 1934–50, produced a significant collection of well-constructed dramas of balanced themes. Although Dr. Valbuena in 1956 judged Casona "the superior dramatist in every respect," [10] the prevailing critical opinion still strongly favors García Lorca. Lorca's native talent was surely superior to Casona's, as was his ability to profoundly move an audience. Lorca's reputation as a dramatist seems assured, but it is still too early to predict whether Casona's reputation relative to Lorca's will improve. Perhaps ultimately Lorca's drama will be considered as representative of the period just prior to the Civil War, Casona's of the years following it.

Inasmuch as the critics have cast Lorca as the leader of a renovation of the Spanish theater, we must face the question whether his dramas were a fulfillment of that challenge or a promise which death cut short. With the passing of time and some weakening of the influence of Lorca's personal impact, the small body of his theater may well suggest more of promise than of fulfillment. Of his five major dramas (some critics would say only three), *The Shoemaker's Prodigious Wife*, *Doña Rosita the Spinster* and in part *Yerma* seem basically traditional, although all of them have elements which show his originality. Therefore we are left with only *Blood Wedding* and *The House of Bernarda Alba* as strong examples of renovation. And certainly it is significant that by common critical agreement these plays and Lorca's drama in general have exerted little influence on subsequent playwrights. We hasten to add that the upheaval of the Civil War in 1936–39 disrupted the normal course of events in the theater. When it finally resumed its course after the war, the playwrights faced a much altered situation, and have followed other influences.

As our discussions have revealed, the distinctive characteristic of Lorca's theater in general is that it is one of memorable and dominant female characters, women who one and all struggle with overwhelming frustrations. Thus the Shoemaker's Wife and Doña Rosita represent frustrated romantic love and motherhood; Yerma represents frustration of the maternal instinct; the Bride in *Blood Wedding* and the daughters in *Bernarda Alba* represent frustration of the sexual instinct. These female characters are contrasted with, and indeed frustrated by, a group of male characters who are impotent, ineffective or even absent as members of the cast. Lorca's reasons for this heavy emphasis on the female characters are of course complex. We have provided in the biographical details on Lorca and in the discussions of his poetry some psychological hints as to his personal reasons. In a more general way, Lorca's drama reflects the modern theme now become a commonplace in world drama: the emasculation of the male character and the rising dominance of the female. Very generally, for example, even in Spanish literature it is instructive to offer as a contrast the theater of Lope de Vega in the Golden Age, in which there is a succession of arrogant Spanish *caballeros,* both as lovers and as fathers. In Lorca's theater (as in part in Benavente's earlier drama), the female dominates, but is herself ultimately defeated. While this shift in emphasis seems to indicate cultural decline, decay or pessimism, a meaningful discussion of the ultimate significance of this question would involve an analysis of the state of Western civilization.

Even if Lorca had only limited success in his renovation of the Spanish theater, his major dramas represent an enduring achievement. His outstanding success in the theater during the brief period 1933–35 and the continuing popularity of some of his dramas cannot be questioned. It is possible, however, as García Luengo has somewhat convincingly done in his *Reevaluation of the Theater of García Lorca,* to attack his drama as being a one-sided view of humanity and of Spanish character so seriously limited that the plays will not endure. Admittedly Lorca's theater, as does his poetry, explores the specific area in which vital passions and instincts are struggling desperately for expression. And, in his view, these passions are consistently frustrated, with the ultimate frustration assuming the form of a living death as in *Doña Rosita,* or as real death in *Blood Wedding* and *The House of Bernarda Alba.* Lorca utilized his poetic talent in developing symbols, in re-creating popular traditions, in pointing up an effective plastic scene to emphasize his view of the omnipresence of the tragic. And, if this view of life normally seems somewhat limited, it is frightening to think how his theme of frustration into death had public expression in the chaos of the Spanish Civil War which truncated his own career.

CHAPTER 8

Lorca's Position and Influence

ALTHOUGH Federico García Lorca represents a solid achievement in drama, he will certainly be best remembered as a poet. Having discussed his standing as a dramatist in the preceding chapter, we shall therefore confine our discussion here to his poetry, his position as a poet and his influence. Among the many fine poets of his generation, Lorca stands out clearly but does not overshadow artists of the stature of Rafael Alberti, Pedro Salinas and Jorge Guillén. Lorca's international reputation eclipsed that of the others, perhaps permanently, but the impartial student of Spanish letters will be reluctant to make a definite choice among the four poets. Rafael Alberti, brilliantly talented, began in the neo-popular vein and passed through a surrealist period as did Lorca; afterward, he wrote poetry of social intent through the Civil War period; his themes have been deeply human since that time. Pedro Salinas, also an intellectual, created an unadorned poetry which expresses the concerns of modern man. Lorca once called Salinas' poetry "domestic," and so it is, in a way that Lorca was incapable of understanding. Jorge Guillén was a poet of the senses like Lorca, but there is a striking difference between Guillén's radiance and Lorca's profound turbulence. Guillén's *Canticle* (*Cántico*), which includes almost all his major work, is as magnificent an achievement as the *Gypsy Ballads*. Among 20th century Spanish poets in general the acknowledged masters are still Antonio Machado and Juan Rámon Jiménez.

García Lorca's poetic world was quite different from that of most of the poets of his generation. Lorca was a poet of the five senses, or as he would say, "of the blood." He can be contrasted strongly with Jiménez, for example, who in splendid isolation conceived an abstraction of Beauty, and then strove for the equivalent in poetic terms. Lorca created from the outside inward, not the contrary. For him poetry was something that "walked along the streets," waiting to be seized by the poet. Imagination was the talent for discovering "clear life in the fragments of invisible reality where man moves." And of course the daughter of the imagination was metaphor. But Lorca felt that imagination was limited by reality and needed "objects, landscapes and planets." [1] With this strong sense of reality, the two chief sources of his work were the traditional materials of Andalusia and his own direct experiences.[2] Inevitably all these materials were transformed in the poetic process to express his own personal view of life.

The theme of the poetry of García Lorca followed an insistent and unwavering line toward death, as his critics have emphasized, but we must stress the fact that in the poet death was usually death-in-life, the struggle between his vital passion and those multiple forces which frustrate its expression. Maturing under the influence of surrealism and the beginnings of existentialism, Lorca was of the temperament to assimilate and express the Spanish tradition in the strident, anguished and desperate terms of those attitudes, without penetrating technically into their philosophies. From his beginnings Lorca, like Antonio Machado, was of dark and tragic temperament. In his *Poem of the Cante Jondo* he first projected oblivion with his theme of the directionless rider. Then in the *Gypsy Ballads*, through his gypsy characters he projected vital passion against the repressing and frustrating forces of the world, and ultimately resolved the conflict by surrendering to psychological death. In *Poet in New York* he armed the conflict again from a more personal standpoint, and achieved a partial victory by directing his energies toward social redemption. Around 1930 Lorca apparently decided that he was fated to consume himself in his work, seeking the ideal comrade (perhaps like Whitman) who would share with him the lonely journey. In the *Divan of Tamarit*, Lorca was struggling to endure through bitter resignation; in the *Lament for the Death of a Bullfighter* he made what proved to be his final statement on death.

Thus Lorca followed the pattern of tragic premonition to vital passion overwhelmed by repression and frustration, to bitter resignation, to death as the end of everything. His poetry of death-in-life, of vitality doomed to frustration, and his life, a great promise doomed to extinction, are together a frightening symbol of our times. In his insistence upon death, he seems to have inherited the predilection of the Spanish for the theme of death since the earliest times, as Pedro Salinas has emphasized. But Lorca went beyond Spanish tradition in at least approaching the ancient problem of the artist with a homosexual attitude and his responsibilities to his culture, a problem emphasized by the French man of letters André Gide. It is impossible to ignore the fact that in the last half of our century the homosexual emphasis, with an implied rejection of life, has increasingly begun to plague literature (especially the theater), so much so that even our news magazines have editorialized upon it. Certainly García Lorca at the time of his death was hesitating between a more open approach to the problem and a return to his Spanish Catholic heritage.

To propose Lorca as a major poet presupposes his achievement of a poetic style and form, and what is impressive with him is that he attempted to remake his style after every book. He had barely finished the satisfying poems of the *cante jondo* in 1922 when he began experimenting with the ultraistic manner. Then around 1926 he blended these two manners to produce the style of the *Gypsy Ballads*. While the ballads are in traditional meter, the distinctive feature of the Lorquian style is in its modern metaphor and imagery, achieved by a certain fusion of elements and a shifting of natural forces. Images such as "Soledad, bathe your body/With water of morning larks," or "And other lasses fled in fright/Pursued by their tresses" have the Lorquian ring, and it is this moment in his style which has been most admired and imitated. But in *Poet in New York*, Lorca changed to the sonorous free verse with long lines, alternating with stanzas of loose traditional form; his technique was accompanied by a heavy stress on the use of symbols to express his meaning. In the *Divan of Tamarit* he again changed direction, emerging with a spare form often based on traditional meters subtly varied, together with a use of symbol and image based upon the personal myth from his own earlier poetry. Finally, still developing, in the largely unpublished *Sonnets of Dark Love* he set himself the challenge of creating within the discipline of the sonnet form. Therefore Lorca could boast of a solid achievement in traditional forms, in vanguard forms and in various blendings of the two.

In Spanish literature Lorca's varied achievement assures him a high place. Lorca anthologizes well, in contrast with Jiménez and Machado, so that perhaps no more than twenty of his best poems create a powerful effect. But as with most poets, a selected works is required to project the range of his personality and achievement. The canon of Lorca's major poetry includes the basic lyrics of *Poem of the Cante Jondo,* a few from *Songs; Gypsy Ballads, Poet in New York* and *Divan of Tamarit* all almost intact; and the *Lament for the Death of a Bullfighter.* The fact that this whole selection numbers hardly ninety poems indicates Lorca's concentration. Since he did not introduce a new movement in Spanish poetry, he will probably never have the stature of Garcilaso, Góngora, Darío or Jiménez, but certainly for the modern reader his total achievement places him among the top ten Spanish poets, with a rank no less than fourth among the modern.

The problem of Lorca's influence must be approached carefully. In Spain, Lorca did exert some influence on his younger contemporaries, but this influence cannot be isolated from those Lorca himself was receiving. By 1933 he was writing to the younger Miguel Hernández somewhat as master to pupil. Certainly Lorca influenced Luis Cernuda, a poet of similar but more delicate temperament; Cernuda surely followed Lorca in the note of rebellion which finally broke out openly in the former's poetry. The other Spanish poets were too sophisticated to imitate the manner of *Gypsy Ballads* and never accepted Lorca's surrealist manner. After the Civil War of 1936–39 the Spanish poets returned to formalism and tranquillity, to simple human expression, even to religion, under the varied influence of many poets, among them the sixteenth century Garcilaso and the modern Antonio Machado. We must tentatively conclude that there has been little direct influence by Lorca on later poets in Spain.

In Spanish America the situation has been different. After the publication of the *Gypsy Ballads,* Lorca became extremely popular in Hispanic America, and his visits to Cuba and later to Argentina helped to solidify his reputation. The Colombian critic Rafael Maya[3] declared in 1937 that there was a "Lorquian technique" among the Hispanic American poets and that the appearance of the *Gypsy Ballads* was an event comparable to the publication of Rubén Darío's *modernista* poetry. Among the many poets influenced by Lorca were Carlos Correa in Chile, Miguel Otero Silva in Venezuela, Jorge Zalamea in Colombia, Claudia Lars in Central America and Manuel José Lira in Mexico.[4] While Lorca's manner in the *Gypsy Ballads* was therefore imitated—somewhat superficially—from Chile to Mexico, in many countries his influence helped to stimulate a return to the popular forms such as the ballad and to native traditions somewhat comparable to that of the gypsy in Spain.

There is strong reason to believe that the "universal Andalusian" in 20th century Spanish literature is Federico García Lorca, not Juan Ramón Jiménez, who is often thus designated.[5] While Jiménez' high place in Spanish literature is indeed assured, Lorca is much more representative as a spokesman both for his native Andalusia and for the 20th century Western world. In his person and in his work Lorca constantly expressed that admixture of the exuberant vitality and resigned tragedy, the companionable gayety and profound loneliness and the capacity for simple beliefs matched by religious pessimism which traditionally characterize the Andalusian. And certainly Lorca expressed and lived the alienation of the individual of our times. *Poet in New York*, an intensely personal yet generally applicable document, is an outstanding example of individual isolation from self, family, society and religion. Lorca's work is turbulent, rebellious, bitterly resigned, with a desperate search for meaning and hope; he was clearly a prophet of our times, however the fact is explained. His powerful work exists as the expression of a human spirit in all its complexity; everyone thought him blessed, but he considered himself fated. García Lorca possessed that quality of magnetism in his person and in his work which has gained for him a unique position in the cultural stream of the Western world.

Notes and References

Chapter One

1. Federico García Lorca, *Obras completas* (Madrid, 1960), pp. 1651–1652. Hereafter called *Obras*.

2. Fernando Vázquez Ocaña, *García Lorca* (México, 1957), p. 63.

3. *Obras*, p. 1478.

4. See Rafael Alberti, "Federico García Lorca y la Residencia de Estudiantes," *Revista de Indias* (Bogotá), X (1941), 5–13.

5. Vázquez Ocaña, p. 113.

6. *Obras*, p. 1655.

7. Salvador Dalí, *The Secret Life of Salvador Dalí*, trans. by Haakon Chevalier (New York, 1942), p. 176.

8. *Ibid.*, p. 174.

9. *Ibid.*, p. 203.

10. *Obras*, p. 1611.

11. *Ibid.*, p. 1623.

12. Ana María Dalí, *Salvador Dalí visto por su hermana*, trans. by María Luz Morales (Barcelona, 1949). Lorca is discussed on pages 102–129.

13. *Obras*, p. 1569.

14. *Ibid.*, p. 1571.

15. Vázquez Ocaña, p. 18.

16. Dalí, *The Secret Life*, p. 167.

17. The Biblioteca Nueva began to publish Freud's complete works in 1922. (See José Ortega y Gassett, *Obras completas*, Vol. VI (Madrid, 1955), p. 301.) The *Interpretation of Dreams* was published around August, 1924. (See the review of the book in *Revista de Occidente*, XVI (1924), 161–163.)

18. Vázquez Ocaña, p. 190.

19. *Obras*, p. 1610.

20. Dalí, *The Secret Life*, pp. 202–203.

21. We are discussing only one. The other is "Loneliness," on p. 541 in the *Obras*, in which at one level of meaning the poet predicts his permanent loneliness because Dalí has severed relations with him.

See Jean-Louis Schonberg, *Federico García Lorca, l'homme, l'oeuvre* (Paris, 1956), p. 216.

22. *Obras*, p. 1632.

23. *Ibid.*, p. 1630.

24. Vázquez Ocaña, p. 208.

25. *Obras*, p. 1575.

26. *Ibid.*, p. 1555.

27. John A. Crow, *Federico García Lorca* (Los Angeles, 1945), p. 47.

28. Carlos Morla, *En España con Federico García Lorca* (Madrid, 1957).

29. See Carlos Morla, p. 351, where apparently this young man is identified.

30. Cipriano Rivas Cherif, "La muerte y la pasión de Federico García Lorca," *Excelsior* (México), Jan. 6, 13, 27, 1957.

31. *Obras*, p. 1763.

32. See Gerald Brenan, *The Face of Spain* (New York, 1956), pp. 131–60. Vázquez Ocaña summarizes the basic materials which have appeared on Lorca's death, pp. 364ff.

33. Schonberg, pp. 101–122.

34. Vázquez Ocaña, p. 379.

Chapter Two

1. Juan Chabás has a good summary of these movements in his *Literatura española contemporánea* (Madrid, 1957), pp. 411–421.

2. Guillermo de Torre, *Literatura europea de vanguardia* (Madrid, 1925), pp. 40–45.

3. *Ibid.*, p. 100.

4. *Obras*, p. 1620.

5. Luis Cernuda, *Estudios sobre poesía española* (Madrid, 1957), p. 195.

6. According to Schonberg, p. 173, the Sephardic Jews established the term *cante jondo* (*cante jomtob*) for this type of song. The related type *flamenco* was the song of their Jewish colleagues driven from Flanders.

7. See Manuel de Falla, *Escritos sobre música* (Buenos Aires, 1950) which is a reprint of de Falla's article.

8. Another brief selection of poems from this period was published as *First Songs* (*Primeras canciones*) by Ediciones Héroe, Madrid, 1936.

9. We refer to Freud's essay "Infantile Sexuality," in *Three Contributions to the Theory of Sex*.

10. Felipe Pedrell, *Cancionero musical popular* (Vals, Cataluña, n. d.).

11. Chabás, p. 457, has a fine discussion of this lyric.

12. For example, Vázquez Ocaña, p. 148.

13. Gerardo Diego, *"Canciones," Revista de Occidente,* XVII (1927), pp. 380–384.

Chapter Three

1. The details in this paragraph are from *Obras,* p. 1659.

2. *Ibid.,* p. 1579.

3. Arturo Berenguer-Carísomo, *Las máscaras de Federico García Lorca* (Buenos Aires, 1941), p. 65, defines the central theme of the *Gypsy Ballads* as the *"tirón sexual y la muerte,"* the sexual and death.

4. See Gustavo Correa, *La poesía de Federico García Lorca* (Eugene, Oregon, 1959).

5. Andrés Soria, "El gitanismo de Federico García Lorca," *Insula,* 45(1049), 8.

6. Jean-Paul Clébert, *The Gypsies,* trans. by Charles Duff (New York, 1962), p. 128.

7. See Graciela Palau, *Vida y obra de Juan Ramón Jiménez* (Madrid, 1957), pp. 254–255.

8. See Concha Zardoya, "La técnica metafórica de Federico García Lorca," *RHM,* XX(1954); Jaroslaw Flys, *La técnica metafórica de Federico García Lorca* (Madrid, 1955).

9. Clébert, pp. 98–101.

10. Luis Cernuda, *Estudios sobre poesía española* (Madrid, 1957), p. 215.

11. See, for example, Guillén's comments in *Obras,* pp. xliv ff.

12. Salvador Dalí, *Hidden Faces,* trans. by Haakon Chevalier (New York, 1944), p. 108.

13. *Obras,* p. 544.

14. See Doris Margaret Glasser, "Lorca's 'Burla de Don Pedro a caballo,' " *Hispania,* XLVII (1964), pp. 295–301, for a different interpretation of the ballad.

15. Guillermo Díaz-Plaja, *Federico García Lorca* (Buenos Aires, 1954), p. 135.

16. The reader who finds this conclusion improbable is asked to read the first half of Dalí's *The Secret Life.*

17. Gabriel Miró, *El obispo leproso* (Madrid, 1928), pp. 294 ff.

18. *Obras,* p. 1754.

19. C. M. Bowra, *The Creative Experiment* (London, 1949), p. 211. Bowra has a long chapter devoted to Lorca's *Gypsy Ballads.*

Chapter Four

1. Federico García Lorca, *Poet in New York*, trans. by Ben Belitt (New York, 1955), p. 183.
2. *Ibid.*, Introduction by Angel del Río, p. xxxv.
3. Federico García Lorca, *Poeta en Nueva York* (México, 1940); Federica García Lorca, *Poet in New York and Other Poems*, trans. by Rolfe Humphries (New York, 1940). Although Lorca himself prepared a Spanish text in 1935, there has remained some confusion as to the number of the New York poems and their final arrangement.
4. Angel del Río has written of three crises, including that in the poet's form. See del Río's fine Introduction to Belitt's translation (note 1, above), a penetrating article in general, although del Río at times passes lightly over the personal poems.
5. *Obras*, p. 1673.
6. See Juan Larrea, "Asesinado por el cielo," *Letras de México,* III (1941–1942), pp. 1, 5–6.
7. Jean-Louis Schonberg, p. 217, has pointed out a comparable example in Lorca's poem "Loneliness," a variation of the "Leda and the Swan" theme, in which Lorca is playing with the word "Leda" as an anagram of "Dalí."
8. Salvador Dalí, *The Secret Life*, pp. 216 ff.
9. Lorca, who had given his only copy of "Crucifixion" to a friend, was not able to get it back when he was organizing the poems of *Poet in New York* in 1935. "Crucifixion" therefore belongs in Section VI, as Belitt has indicated. See Belitt's book (note 1, above), pp. 188–189.
10. Cernuda, pp. 216–7.
11. Lorca revealed this idea of the comrade to Rivas Cherif, the director of some of his dramas.
12. Larrea, pp. 1, 5–6.

Chapter Five

1. Emilio García Gómez, *Poesía arabigoandaluza* (Madrid, 1952), p. 91.
2. Guillermo Díaz-Plaja, p. 172.
3. Cernuda, p. 218.
4. *Obras*, p. lxxiv.
5. "Lorca's *Llanto por Ignacio Sánchez Mejías* and the Elegiac Tradition," *Hispanic Review*, XXXI (1963), 229–238.

Chapter Six

1. For a good brief discussion of the theater in this period see Juan Chabás, pp. 605 ff. On the European influences, see Arturo Berenguer-Carísomo, pp. 113 ff.

Notes and References

2. *Obras*, pp. 1657–1658.
3. See Sumner M. Greenfield, "The Problem of *Mariana Pineda*," *Massachusetts Review*, I (1960), 751–759.
4. Jean-Louis Schonberg, pp. 287–91.
5. See Manuel Durán, "El surrealismo en el teatro de García Lorca y de Alberti," *Hispanófila*, I (1957), 60–64.
6. *Obras*, p. 1679.

Chapter Seven

1. See the Introduction in English to Federico García Lorca, *La zapatera prodigiosa*, ed. Edith F. Helman (New York, 1952).
2. *Obras*, pp. 1694–6.
3. Alfredo de la Guardia, *García Lorca, persona y creación* (Buenos Aires, 1944), pp. 379 ff., has a sensitive discussion of *Doña Rosita*.
4. Alfredo de la Guardia, pp. 350–351.
5. Edward C. Riley, "Sobre *Bodas de Sangre*," *Clavileño*, VII (1951), 8–12.
6. Angel Valbuena Prat, *Historia del Teatro Español* (Barcelona, 1956), p. 641.
7. Angel del Río, p. 247.
8. *Obras*, p. 1759.
9. Roberto Sánchez, *García Lorca: estudio sobre su teatro* (Madrid, 1950), p. 68.
10. Valbuena Prat, p. 634.

Chapter Eight

1. *Obras*. We are extracting from the two articles on pages 1543 and 1755.
2. The reader may profitably consult Angel del Río, pp. 252–259, for some profound conclusions on Lorca and his work.
3. Rafael Maya, "García Lorca," *Revista de Indias* (Bogotá), I (1936–7), 26–28. John A. Crow, pp. 105–112, has many details on Lorca's influence in Hispanic America.
4. Crow, pp. 111–112.
5. Manuel Durán, "García Lorca, poeta entre dos mundos," *Asomante*, XVII (1962), 76, has called Lorca the "universal Andalusian," but develops the idea with details different from ours.

Selected Bibliography

PRIMARY SOURCES
(Short publications are omitted.)

Impresiones y paisajes. Granada: Tipografía P. V. Traveset, 1918.

Libro de poemas. Madrid: Maroto, 1921.

Canciones. Málaga: Litoral, 1927.

Primer romancero gitano. Madrid: Revista de Occidente, 1928.

Poema del cante jondo. Madrid: C. I. A. P., 1931.

Llanto por Ignacio Sánchez Mejías. Madrid: Ed. del Arbol, 1935.

El diván del Tamarit. New York: *Revista Hispánica Moderna,* VII (1940), pp. 307–312.

Poeta en Nueva York. México: Editorial Séneca, 1940.

Mariana Pineda. Madrid: Rivadeneyra, 1928.

Bodas de Sangre. Madrid: Cruz y Raya, 1935.

Yerma. Buenos Aires: Ed. Anaconda, 1937.

Obras completas. Buenos Aires: Losada, 1938–1946, 8 vols. Lorca's other important dramas were generally first published in this edition. *La zapatera prodigiosa* is in vol. III, *Doña Rosita la soltera* in vol. V, *Así que pasen cinco años* in vol. VI, *La casa de Bernarda Alba* in vol. VIII, 1946.

Obras completas. Madrid: Aguilar, 1954. Other editions, 1957, 1960, 1965. The definitive edition of Lorca's work, although *Impresiones y paisajes* is printed only in fragments.

SECONDARY SOURCES

Alonso, Dámaso. *Poetas españoles contemporáneos.* Madrid: Editorial Gredos, 1952. Important source materials on Lorca's generation of poets.

Babín, María Teresa. *García Lorca, vida y obra.* New York: Las Américas, 1955. Substantial criticism of a traditional nature.

Barea, Arturo. *Lorca: the Poet and His People,* trans. by Isla Barea. New York: Harcourt-Brace, 1958. Important for Lorca's Andalusian traditions.

Berenguer-Carísomo, Arturo. *Las máscaras de Federico García Lorca.* Buenos Aires: Ruiz Hermanos, 1941. Much on the European background of Lorca's work; important criticism.

Bowra, C. M. *The Creative Experiment.* London: Macmillan, 1949. Chapter VII is devoted to a meaningful (even though at times superficial) analysis of the *Gypsy Ballads.*

Campbell, Roy. *Lorca: An Appreciation of his Poetry.* New Haven: Yale Press, 1952. Includes much of Lorca's poetry in Campbell's translation.

Cernuda, Luis. *Estudios sobre poesía española.* Madrid: Ediciones Guadarrama, 1957. A sober evaluation of Lorca's poetry.

Chabás, Juan. *Literatura española contemporánea.* La Habana: Cultural, S. A., 1952. Good source material for the whole period.

Correa, Gustavo. *La poesía mítica de Federico García Lorca.* Eugene, Oregon: U. of Oregon Press, 1957. A competent study with meaningful criticism of individual poems.

Crow, John A. *Federico García Lorca.* Los Angeles: U. of California Press, 1945. Important for Lorca's stay in New York, his influence on Hispanic America poets.

Dalí, Salvador. *The Secret Life,* trans. by Haakon Chevalier. New York: Dial Press, 1942. Very important for understanding Lorca's revolutionary attitudes.

Díaz-Plaja, Guillermo. *Federico García Lorca; su obra e influencia en la poesía española.* Buenos Aires: Espasa Calpe, 1954. Competent (but at times evasive) criticism by a fine critic.

Flys, Jaroslaw. *El lenguaje poético de Federico García Lorca.* Madrid: Editorial Gredos, 1955. Fine study of emblem, metaphor and symbol in Lorca's poetry.

García-Luengo, Eusebio. *Revisión del teatro de Federico García Lorca.* Madrid: Cuadernos de Política y Literatura, 1951. Brief but important negative criticism of Lorca's theater.

de la Guardia, Alfredo. *García Lorca, persona y creación.* Buenos Aires: Editorial Schapire, 1944. Somewhat "poetic," but sensitive criticism, especially of Lorca's drama.

Guillén, Jorge. *Federico en persona.* Buenos Aires: Emecé, 1959. Personal reminiscences of Lorca.

Honig, Edwin. *García Lorca.* Norfolk, Connecticut: New Directions, 1944. A well-written book with the traditional approach to Lorca.

Lima, Robert. *The Theatre of García Lorca.* New York: Las Américas, 1963.

Lorca, A Collection of Critical Essays, ed. Manuel Durán. Englewood Cliffs, N.J.: Prentice-Hall, 1962.

Morla Lynch, Carlos. *En España con Federico García Lorca.* Madrid:

Selected Bibliography

Aguilar, 1957. Important biographical source for the years 1931–1936.

del Río, Angel. "Federico García Lorca." *Revista Hispánica Moderna,* VII (1940).

Sánchez, Roberto. *García Lorca, estudio sobre su teatro.* Madrid: Ediciones Jura, 1950. Penetrating (although brief) analysis of Lorca's individual plays.

Schonberg, Jean-Louis. *Federico García Lorca, l'homme, l'oeuvre.* Paris: Librairie Plon, 1956. Important biographical details; valuable penetration of Lorca's work.

de Torre, Guillermo. *Literatura española de vanguardia.* Madrid: R. Caro Raggio, 1925. Basic source of history of *ultraísmo,* literary background.

Vázquez Ocaña, Fernando. *García Lorca.* México: Biografías Gandesa, 1957. Important biographical details; criticism and conclusions somewhat weak.

Valbuena Prat, Angel. *Historia del teatro español.* Barcelona: Editorial Noguer, 1956. The standard history of the Spanish Theater. For Lorca, see pp. 633–651.

Zardoya, Concha. "La técnica metafórica de Federico García Lorca. *Revista Hispánica Moderna,* IV (1954), pp. 295–326. Indicates the richness of Lorca's poetic forms.

Index

(Lorca's works are listed under the English title.)

[158]

Index